1985.

WHO SHOT J.R. . . . AND WHO *BIT* J.R.?

WHO WAS PAM'S FIRST HUSBAND?

WHICH ACTRESS CREATED THE ROLE OF JENNA WADE?

HOW MUCH MONEY DID JOCK LEAVE LUCY?

The rich and the powerful, the good and the evil, the innocent and the very, very guilty - they're all here in this memory-teasing collection of 144 quizzes about your favourite *Dallas* characters and their best (and worst) moments on the screen.

D1638233

T·H·E O·F·F·I·C·I·A·L

BALLAS™

TRIVIA BOOK

JASON BONDEROFF

**Based on the Series by
David Jacobs**

A STAR BOOK
published by
the Paperback Division of
W. H. Allen & Co. PLC

A Star Book
Published in 1985
by the Paperback Division of
W. H. Allen & Co. PLC
44 Hill Street, London, W1X 8LB

First published in the United Stated of America by the
New American Library, 1984.
Published by arrangement with the New American Library,
New York, NY.

Copyright © 1984 by Jason Bonderoff

Printed and bound in Great Britain by
Anchor Brendon Ltd. Tiptree, Essex

ISBN 0 352 31717 5

All quotations, elements and underlying material derived from
the television series *Dallas*™ copyright © 1978, 1984
Lorimar Productions, Inc. All rights reserved. Licensed by Lorimar
Licensing Co.

Dallas,™ 'J.R.'™, 'Ewing'™, and 'Southfork Ranch'™ are trademarks
of Lorimar Productions, Inc. All rights reserved.

The *Dallas* Series ™ & © 1978, 1984 by Lorimar Productions.
All rights reserved. Licensed by Lorimar Licensing Co.

This book is sold subject to the condition that it
shall not, by way of trade or otherwise, be lent,
resold, hired out, or otherwise circulated without
the publisher's prior consent in any form of binding
or cover other than that in which it is published and
without a similar condition including this condition
being imposed on the subsequent purchaser.

Introduction

When *Dallas* premiered on April 2, 1978, we didn't know if we'd struck oil or merely hit rock bottom. Certainly, our show was new and different and a major departure from most primetime drama, but would it succeed? Were viewers ready to accept a feisty, super-rich family called the Ewings who thrived on power and ambition? Jock and Miss Ellie and their two sons, Bobby and J.R., were hardly the average clan next door. They were light years removed from the 1950's family—and just about every other family who'd ever been invited into the living rooms of TV-viewing America.

Ultimately, that's what made *Dallas* a hit. We dared to be different—we dared to portray human beings who were both weak and strong; loving and ruthless—and audiences responded enthusiastically. Our cast is perhaps the most three-dimensional group of characters ever assembled. Each one is an intriguing mixture of sinner and saint; no one is perfect, but everyone is human.

In fact, human triumph mixed with human frailty is the thread linking everything that happens in *Dallas*. The Barnes and the Ewings play for high stakes and often pay a high price for their follies, but through it all they remain fighters. Even when we can't applaud their motives, we admire their spirit.

This book reminds me of some of the show's most exciting moments. Sue Ellen's secret love affair with Cliff, the paternity battle over John Ross, the shooting of J.R., the courtship of Ray and Donna, Bobby and J.R.'s year-long contract for control of Ewing Oil, and the bittersweet breakup of Pam and Bobby's marriage. Over the years, I've welcomed new cast members like Susan Howard, Howard Keel and Priscilla Beaulieu Presley to the family fold. Donna Reed has recently taken over as Miss Ellie. Of course, for all of us, the saddest time of all, was the death of Jim Davis in 1981. We knew then there could never be another Jock Ewing.

Nearly seven years ago, when Bobby showed up at Southfork with his nervous bride Pamela, a brand-new era in primetime programming was born. Whether you've been a Dallas fan from the beginning or tuned into the doings of the Ewings in syndicated rerun, you'll find this book delightfully challenging. There are even a few mind-benders tricky enough to stump J.R.!

Leonard Katzman, Producer
October, 1984

T·H·E
O·F·F·I·C·I·A·L
BALLAS™
TRIVIA
BOOK

Welcome to Southfork

Quiz 1
The Southfork Scene

1. Who said, "It's wonderful how thoughtful he can be when he's caught with his choo-choo in the wrong tunnel"? Who was the subject of that remark?
2. What is Cliff Barnes's favorite kind of food?
3. How much does a ticket to the Oil Barons' Ball cost?
4. Where was Sue Ellen's mother when J. R. was shot?
5. How long were Pam and Bobby married?
6. Which three actresses have played the role of Jenna Wade?
7. Who was Amanda Ewing's husband? What happened to Amanda?
8. Who bought a house in Biloxi for her mother?
9. Who was Bobby Ewing's Canadian Santa Claus—and how much money did he bring him?
10. What happened on March 21, 1980?

9

The Stars Shine Bright

Quiz 2
The Southfork Scene

Name the actor or actress who made each of these roles famous.

1. Bobby Ewing
2. Pamela Ewing
3. J. R. Ewing
4. Jock Ewing
5. Ellie Ewing (1978–84)
6. Sue Ellen Ewing
7. Lucy Ewing
8. Ray Krebbs
9. Cliff Barnes
10. Donna Krebbs
11. Clayton Farlow
12. Ellie Farlow (1984–   )

Southfork Siring Squad

Quiz 3
The Southfork Scene

Who are the natural parents of each of these characters?

1. Bobby Ewing
2. Pamela Ewing
3. Charlie Wade
4. J. R. Ewing
5. John Ross Ewing III
6. Christopher Ewing
7. Cliff Barnes
8. Katherine Wentworth
9. Lucy Ewing
10. Ray Krebbs

Yesterday's Memories

Quiz 4
The Southfork Scene

Bobby once told Pam that their feelings for each other were only "yesterday's memories." Here are a few other couples who might second that emotion. Just match them up.

Column A
1. Kristin Shepard
2. Liz Craig
3. Julie Grey
4. Pamela Ewing
5. Sue Ellen Ewing
6. Garnet McGee
7. Ellie Ewing
8. Donna Krebbs
9. Evelyn Michaelson
10. Valene Ewing

Column B
a. Jock Ewing
b. Gary Ewing
c. Alex Ward
d. Rudy Millington
e. Paul Morgan
f. Ray Krebbs
g. Harrison Page
h. Mitch Cooper
i. Dusty Farlow
j. Frank Crutcher

Spouse Hunting

Quiz 5
The Southfork Scene

In each case fill in the spouse's first name.

 1. Dusty and _____ Farlow
 2. Walt and _____ Driscoll
 3. Edgar and _____ Randolph
 4. Punk and _____ Anderson
 5. Clint and _____ Ogden
 6. Jessica and _____ Montford
 7. Seth and _____ Stone
 8. Amos and _____ Krebbs
 9. Craig and _____ Stewart
10. Henry and _____ Webster

Name Dropping

Quiz 6
The Southfork Scene

Match the ladies with the maiden or married names they dropped along the way.

Column A
1. Ellie Farlow
2. Donna Krebbs
3. Jessica Montford
4. Lucy Ewing
5. Rebecca Wentworth
6. Sue Ellen Ewing
7. Valene Ewing
8. Pamela Barnes
9. Jenna Wade
10. Kristin Shepard

Column B
a. Cooper
b. Haynes
c. Farraday
d. Culver
e. Southworth
f. Marchetta
g. Farlow
h. Barnes
i. Shepard
j. Clements

Ranchers, Riggers, and Rascals

Quiz 7
The Southfork Scene

1. On what road is Southfork located?
2. What annual family gathering is a Ewing tradition?
3. What character has suffered two miscarriages?
4. When Cliff was arrested for shooting J. R., what did he do in the police station?
5. What foursome spent a carefree afternoon at Six Flags Amusement Park?
6. What is Sue Ellen's favorite shade of roses?
7. Who was J. R. criticizing when he said, "Darlin', I do not take kindly to little girls from out of state calling me stupid"?
8. What actress won an Emmy for her *Dallas* role?
9. What does DOA stand for?
10. What two companies, besides Barnes/Wentworth, successfully bid for government offshore oil tracts?

Southfork . . . The Story Continues

Quiz 8
The Southfork Scene

1. Who was Mrs. Chambers?
2. What crucial mistake did both Holly Harwood and Katherine Wentworth make?
3. Who opened a chain of cut-rate gas stations?
4. Who tried to jump off Reunion Tower?
5. Why did Marilee Stone once sue the Ewings? How much did she seek in damages?
6. Who said, "I'm still the same size, just a couple of million dollars lighter"?
7. What tragic event did Miss Ellie believe was the cause of Pam and Bobby's breakup?
8. Who cheated Uncle Jonas out of his potentially profitable oil land?
9. Where were Pam and Bobby when J. R. was shot? How did the news finally reach them?
10. Who was Aunt Maggie?

Dallas Dilemmas

Quiz 9
The Southfork Scene

1. What was Mickey Trotter's hometown?
2. When Peter Richards's college buddies saw Sue Ellen, who did they think she was?
3. Where did Katherine Wentworth reside in Dallas?
4. Who was Annie?
5. What Dallas law firm did Alan Beam work for?
6. What character underwent coronary bypass surgery?
7. Which of Sue Ellen's lovers became impotent?
8. What was the name of Cliff's consortium?
9. What wilderness preserve did Jock and Ellie fight over?
10. Who played matchmaker in Punk and Mavis's romance?

They All Loved Lucy

Quiz 10
The Southfork Scene

Column A lists ten men who have figured prominently in Lucy's life. You'll find the appropriate description for each man in column B.

Column A
1. Alan Beam
2. Roger Larson
3. Mitch Cooper
4. Philip Colton
5. Kit Mainwaring
6. Blair Sullivan
7. Peter Richards
8. Bill Johnson
9. Greg Forrester
10. Mickey Trotter

Column B
a. John Ross brought them together
b. married prof who should have taught motel management
c. Lucy's first broken engagement
d. her rough-and-tumble Kansas conquest
e. medical student who resented her money
f. Kristin was her rival
g. he snapped her up with tragic consequences
h. Lucy's modeling agent
i. lawyer who handled her divorce
j. client's son who wanted to mix business with pleasure

Can You Relate to That?

Quiz 11
The Southfork Scene

How many of these Barnes, Ewing, and Farlow clan members can you identify?

 1. Ellie's newly acquired sister-in-law
 2. Lucy's maternal grandmother
 3. Dave Culver's stepmom
 4. Lil Trotter's nephew
 5. Christopher's maternal aunt
 6. Miss Ellie's oldest son
 7. Lucy's stepmother
 8. Jock's niece
 9. Afton's brother
10. John Ross's youngest uncle

More Strained Relations

Quiz 12
The Southfork Scene

Who are these occasionally, regularly, or formerly featured *Dallas* relatives?

1. John Baxter's father-in-law
2. Thornton McLeish's brother
3. Miss Ellie's brother
4. Afton's mother
5. Clayton's son
6. John Ross's younger cousin
7. John Ross's older cousin
8. Lil's son
9. Harry McSween's "niece"
10. Katherine's ex-brother-in-law

Not-So-Happily-Ever Afton

Quiz 13
The Southfork Scene

Each of these characters has in some way influenced Afton's bittersweet life. Do you know them all?

1. Afton warned Pam not to trust her
2. He only proposed marriage once—and then he mumbled it
3. Her death meant a little windfall for Afton
4. He was unrefined, but his bed led directly to a refinery for Cliff
5. Afton's best friend in Dallas
6. He lured her upstairs on Lucy's wedding day
7. His marriage brought her to Dallas
8. His pool was her favorite place for a Sunday swim
9. Afton came home—and found her in Cliff's arms
10. Afton wanted to save his marriage

The Cowboy's Wife

Quiz 14
The Southfork Scene

1. In what city was Donna born?
2. What happened to her parents?
3. Who was her first husband? What past political offices had he held?
4. How did Donna and Miss Ellie become friends?
5. Where were Ray and Donna married?
6. Who were their witnesses?
7. Where did they spend their honeymoon?
8. What nearly caused their first marital squabble?
9. As an author, what kind of books does Donna write?
10. Who was the subject of her most successful book?

Sue Ellen's Suitors

Quiz 15
The Southfork Scene

Sue Ellen seems to drift from man to man as casually as some women change their hairstyles—but she always comes back to J. R. Can you identify each of these lovers and/or friends?

1. Her first husband
2. Her second husband
3. Her rodeo-loving Romeo
4. The boy she skipped cheerleading practice for
5. He *always* listened when Sue Ellen spoke
6. Talk-show host who took a shine to her
7. He's not one of the world's biggest spenders
8. Her youngest conquest
9. Her not quite fatherly friend
10. The lawyer who helped her win custody of John Ross

In The Beginning . . .

Quiz 16
The Southfork Scene

Dallas premiered on April 2, 1978, as a five-part miniseries, then became a weekly program in September 1978. Quizzes 15–20 will help conjure up memories of *Dallas'* first five shows.

1. In the very first episode Pam had just:
   a. married Bobby;
   b. suffered a miscarriage;
   c. been reunited with her mother.
2. The title of the first episode referred specifically to Pam. It was called:
   a. "The New Mrs. Ewing";
   b. "The Homecoming";
   c. "Digger's Daughter."
3. In the opening show J. R.'s secretary was:
   a. Connie;
   b. Louella;
   c. Julie.
4. Pam was pushed into a lake by:
   a. Bobby;
   b. J. R.;
   c. Ray.
5. Bobby was in charge of Ewing Oils':
   a. advertising;
   b. public relations;
   c. off-shore drilling operations.

6. Jock's nickname for J. R. was:
   a. J. R.;
   b. Junior;
   c. Johnny.
7. Lucy was secretly:
   a. cutting classes;
   b. taking acting lessons;
   c. visiting Cliff Barnes.
8. The counsel to the legislative committee investigating the Ewings was:
   a. Roger Perry;
   b. Buzz Connors;
   c. Cliff Barnes.
9. The character first called "Greg," then "Carl," later appeared on screen as:
   a. Gary Ewing;
   b. Dusty Farlow;
   c. Ray Krebbs.
10. Pam and Bobby were married in:
    a. Dallas;
    b. Las Vegas;
    c. New Orleans.

Heroes, Hustlers, and Heels

Quiz 17
The Southfork Scene

For each man in Column A, find the appropriate description in Column B.

Column A
1. Luther Frick
2. Cliff Barnes
3. Bill Orloff
4. Roger Perry
5. Digger Barnes
6. Jock Ewing
7. Ray Krebbs
8. Jimmy Monahan
9. Bobby Ewing
10. J. R. Ewing

Column B
a. he bought Bobby a Shetland pony
b. Lucy's imitation "hayseed"
c. still carried a torch for Pam
d. vengeful husband who held the Ewings hostage
e. the Ewings bribed him with a house
f. he reminded Lucy of her father
g. Julie charmed him with a smile—and a file
h. a very disinterested husband
i. he tried to blackmail Lucy into making love
j. was his wife a spy?

Missing Persons

Quiz 18
The Southfork Scene

Complete each statement by filling in the name of the appropriate character (or characters).

1. After _____ retired, _____ became chief executive of Ewing Oil.
2. _____ reminded Miss Ellie of herself as a young woman.
3. _____ was in love with J. R. long before he married _____.
4. _____ spent his twenties dispensing broads, booze, and booty for Ewing Oil.
5. Jock and Ellie's ranch foreman was _____.
6. As a teenager, _____ used to break windows in the Ewing Oil office building.
7. Julie Grey was sexually intimate with both _____ and J.R.
8. Pam tried to take charge of _____ as a way to get close to _____ and win her approval.
9. _____ and _____ spent a memorable night with Wanda Frick and Mary Lou Allen in a Waco motel.
10. J. R. questioned the paternity of _____'s baby.
11. Pam felt excluded when _____ and _____ went shopping in Dallas.
12. _____ claimed that a man named Miller had tried to rape her.
13. Two of Pam's relatives had been college classmates. They were _____ and _____.
14. _____ and _____ were in downtown Dallas when the hurricane struck.
15. Lucy had been separated from her mother by _____.

Personal Touches

Quiz 19
The Southfork Scene

1. Miss Ellie occasionally suffered from _____.
2. Sue Ellen tried to spark J. R.'s romantic interest with a _____.
3. In college Cliff had worked as a _____.
4. Lucy loved to entertain her boyfriends in the _____.
5. J. R. accused Pam of stealing his secret _____.
6. When Pam bought Lucy a new _____, she threw it out the car window.
7. Lucy burned a _____ from her high school guidance counselor.
8. Ray offered to give Pam a tour of Southfork by _____.
9. The empty room in J. R. and Sue Ellen's wing of the house was a _____.
10. J. R. wanted to send Bobby to _____ to squelch the legislature's investigation of Ewing Oil.
11. A _____ in Bobby's office revealed that Julie Grey and Cliff Barnes weren't strangers.
12. The constant noise in Bobby's office was caused by _____.

The First Barbecue

Quiz 20
The Southfork Scene

1. Who were Sam and Tillie?
2. Who was Willard—and who was unhappy to see him at the Southfork barbecue?
3. What announcement made Sue Ellen get drunk?
4. Why couldn't Digger toast Pam's happy news?
5. What two things of Digger's had Jock supposedly stolen?
6. How old was Miss Ellie when she and Digger had been sweethearts?
7. In 1930, who had saved Southfork from financial ruin? What was his reward?
8. How did Pam suffer a miscarriage?
9. Who did Bobby hold responsible for Pam's accident?
10. Who convinced Pam not to leave Southfork?

Wild, Wild Guests

Quiz 21
1978–79 Season

During its first full season on the air *Dallas* featured many exciting guest stars. Here are some of the characters they immortalized. How many of the performers can you remember?

1. Gary Ewing
2. Val Ewing
3. Digger Barnes
4. Garnet McGee
5. Kristin Shepard
6. Julie Grey
7. Mrs. Shepard
8. Leanne
9. Liz Craig
10. Willie Gust

"My Three Sons—Ewing Style"

Quiz 22
1978–79 Season

1. Name Jock and Ellie's three sons.
2. Who was the oldest? Who was the youngest?
3. Which of the boys suffered from shyness as a child?
4. Who was Gary named after?
5. Who was Jock's favorite?
6. Who was Miss Ellie's favorite?
7. What kind of car did J. R. drive? How did his license plate read?
8. Which Ewing son became a blackjack dealer in Las Vegas?
9. One of the boys had been Donna's college classmate. Any guesses?
10. Who wanted to build a shopping center on Southfork?
11. Which of her sons did Miss Ellie describe as "the Southworth among Ewings"?
12. Who helped Garnet McGee get a recording contract?
13. Which of Jock's boys originally wanted to be a painter?
14. Who was kidnapped and held for $1,500,000 ransom?
15. Whom did Cliff Barnes describe as "Texas's answer to Michael Corleone"?

Family Matters

Quiz 23
1978–79 Season

1. What two family members were backgammon enthusiasts? When they played, who invariably lost?
2. What was the color of Bobby's Mercedes? How did his license plate read?
3. What were Sue Ellen's two favorite poolside hobbies?
4. Who played the guitar?
5. Who had supposedly quit smoking but was always sneaking off somewhere to take a few secret puffs?
6. What did Sue Ellen keep in a shoe box on the top shelf of her closet?
7. What kind of car did Pam drive?
8. Miss Ellie was devoted to Southfork, but what did she love even more than the land?
9. Who was president of the Daughters of the Alamo?
10. What family member got hooked on Quaaludes?
11. Why did Sue Ellen decide to paint the nursery pale yellow?
12. Who drove too fast?
13. Bobby had achieved distinction in what college sport?
14. Who was Harlan Danvers?
15. Miss Ellie admitted she had once used a horsewhip. For what purpose?

Fast Times at Braddock High

Quiz 24
1978–79 Season

1. Lucy's middle name is _____.
2. Her worst subject in high school was _____.
3. Kit Mainwaring couldn't go through with his marriage to Lucy because _____.
4. Lucy went to a diner in Fort Worth to find _____.
5. Pam and Bobby's graduation present to Lucy was _____.
6. Shocking as it now seems, Lucy's occasional cowboy lover was _____.
7. When Lucy was kidnapped by Willie Gust, she missed her own _____.
8. The family member who kept pushing Lucy and Kit Mainwaring together was _____.
9. Lucy's favorite aunt was _____.
10. Laurence Templeton took Lucy to _____.
11. Lucy occasionally dated Pam's nephew _____.
12. According to Lucy, when she told her grandparents that she wanted to become a singer, they reacted as if she'd said _____.

Rich Girls, Poor Girls

Quiz 25
1978–79 Season

Match the ladies in Column A with the phrases in Column B that describe them best.

Column A
1. Rita Briggs
2. Leann Rees
3. Jennifer Ames
4. Cathy Baker
5. Jenna Wade
6. Fay Parker
7. Anita Krane
8. Kristin Shepard
9. Cora Kincaid
10. Garnet McGee

Column B
a. Sue Ellen's DOA buddy
b. this architecturel student had designs on Bobby
c. Maynard Anderson's mistress
d. one of Bobby's kidnappers
e. the Mustang Club's main attraction
f. her baby was for sale
g. Garrison Southworth's companion
h. former call girl
i. the first girl Cliff ever loved
j. Sue Ellen's obstetrician

Scamps, Tramps, and Scoundrels

Quiz 26
1978–79 Season

Match the rascals in Column A with the phrases in Column B that describe them best.

Column A
1. Ben Maxwell
2. Will Hart
3. Dan Marsh
4. Willy Joe Garr
5. Harrison Slade
6. Taylor Bennett
7. Buzz Connors
8. Bill Orloff
9. Wayne Jessup
10. Hatton

Column B
a. Lucy's drug supplier
b. corrupt senator backed by J. R.
c. arranged black market adoptions
d. Sue Ellen's sanitarium bartender
e. J. R.'s private detective
f. one of Bobby's kidnappers
g. Cliff's political backer
h. Jeb Ames's unsavory partner
i. construction scams were his forte
j. Cliff's opponent, forced to drop out of the race for state senator

Secrets

Quiz 27
1978–79 Season

1. Why did Miss Ellie's brother, Garrison, return to Southfork?
2. What did the infamous "red file" contain? Who stole it?
3. What had happened to Pam in Juarez, Mexico, in 1968?
4. Who did Ray meet at the Longhorn Bar? Why did that shock Pam and Bobby?
5. How did Pam wind up on the front page of the *Dallas Press*? Was the allegation true?
6. What part of Cliff's past came back to haunt him when he ran for state senator?
7. Who did Ray find in Garnet McGee's apartment?
8. How did Pam figure out that Cliff was having an affair with Sue Ellen?
9. Where was J. R. when his parents called to say Sue Ellen was pregnant?
10. Why did J. R. *really* want Sue Ellen locked away in a sanitarium?

Digging Deeper

Quiz 28
1978–79 Season

1. How much money was J. R. worth in 1978?
2. Who was appointed head of the Office of Land Management?
3. On his return to Southfork, what did Garrison bring Miss Ellie?
4. To what sanitarium was Sue Ellen admitted?
5. Who told Bobby "never to get romantic before noon on Saturday"?
6. Who were Chris and Marjorie?
7. What do J. R., Bobby, and Pam never have time for?
8. What did Bobby bring along on the one occasion when he dined with Cliff?
9. Why was Pam supposed to go to Paris?
10. The two-part episode titled "Reunion" focused on which two characters?
11. Who lived at 4524 East Hobart Place?
12. On what was Sue Ellen eager to spend $15,000?
13. Who was Patricia?
14. Who was Amber?
15. In the closing episode of the first season, the very last line of dialogue was: "She has to live . . . damn it . . . she has to live." Who said it? About whom?

Sue Ellen and Cliff

Quiz 29
1978–79 Season

1. Sue Ellen and Cliff met:
   a. outside a Dallas restaurant;
   b. at Southfork;
   c. at The Store.
2. Cliff's first words to her were:
   a. "Do you come here often?";
   b. "If you're J. R.'s wife, we have nothing to say";
   c. "You're much too pretty to be a Ewing."
3. Sue Ellen, in turn, told Cliff, "You're much more attractive than:
   a. your campaign posters";
   b. your reputation";
   c. you give yourself credit for."
4. Sue Ellen's mother urged her to:
   a. leave J. R.;
   b. have an abortion;
   c. be a good wife to J. R.
5. Cliff's arrest for the murder of Julie Grey indirectly caused;
   a. Pam and Bobby's separation;
   b. Sue Ellen and J. R.'s reconciliation;
   c. John Ross's premature birth.
6. When Pam found out about her sister-in-law's affair, she:
   a. told Bobby;
   b. asked Miss Ellie's advice;
   c. kept silent.

7. Sue Ellen eventually confessed everything to:
   a. Miss Ellie;
   b. her sister;
   c. Bobby.
8. The family realized that Sue Ellen's drinking had become uncontrollable when she:
   a. fell down a flight of stairs;
   b. tried to set Southfork on fire;
   c. refused to leave her room.
9. When John Ross was born:
   a. Jock vowed to disinherit the child;
   b. Cliff vowed to raise him like a Barnes;
   c. Pam had a breakdown.
10. J. R. believed that John Ross:
    a. was his child;
    b. was not his child;
    c. had been fathered by Bobby.

"The Red File"

Quiz 30
1978–79 Season

Julie Grey, a former Ewing Oil secretary, stole J. R.'s infamous "red file" and was later murdered for it. The file contained a number of sensational documents that incriminated both J. R. and his sleazy business cohorts, Jeb Ames and Willy Joe Garr. Cliff Barnes was arrested for the murder, but a letter—mailed by Julie just a few hours before her death—eventually helped set him free. See if you can recall these details about Cliff's trial.

1. Why did the police think Cliff had murdered Julie?
2. What was the leading piece of evidence against him?
3. How did the police misinterpret that evidence—and what was its real meaning?
4. Where had Julie hidden the "red file"?
5. What was in the letter she had sent to Cliff?
6. How did Julie actually die?
7. Who was responsible for her death?
8. Who was Lyle Sloan? Who was Cole Young?
9. Cliff had been involved with the "red file" once before. In what way?
10. After the trial what part of the file did Bobby burn?

Wish I'd Said That . . .

Identify the characters who uttered these priceless, and occasionally prophetic, remarks.

1. "A good secretary is harder to find than a good wife."
2. "They [Jeb Ames and Willy Joe Garr] wouldn't attend their own mothers' funerals unless they thought the undertaker'd strike oil."
3. "I've never known Jenna [Wade] to show up and not cause trouble."
4. "I hear nobody goes to the john less you give the okay."
5. "What's so upsetting about being a Ewing and having money? It never sent me to a sanitarium."
6. "His wife treats him like a child. . . . I treat him like a man."
7. "One day I'll learn the rules you play by—and then I'll pay you back."
8. "You're not with one of the world's big spenders now."
9. "The sooner I wash away the smell of him, the better off I'll be."
10. "The Ewings destroy everything they get their hands on. . . . If you live with vipers you become one."

Title Characters

Quiz 32
1978–79 Season

Column A lists the titles of ten *Dallas* episodes. Match each title with the character (in Column B) to whom the title refers.

Column A
1. "Old Acquaintance"
2. "Bypass"
3. "Kidnapped"
4. "Election"
5. "Fallen Idol"
6. "Runaway"
7. "The Outsider"
8. "Call Girl"
9. "Home Again"
10. "Sue Ellen's Sister"

Column B
a. Kristin Shepard
b. Donna Culver
c. Jenna Wade
d. Lucy Ewing
e. Garrison Southworth
f. Jock Ewing
g. Cliff Barnes
h. Bobby Ewing
i. Taylor "Guzzler" Bennett
j. Leann Rees

Wild, Wild Guests

Quiz 33
1979–80 Season

A number of new faces took command of the *Dallas* scene during the 1979–80 season. Can you recall the actor or actress who portrayed each of these characters?

1. Alan Beam
2. Kristin Shepard
3. Digger Barnes
4. Dusty Farlow
5. Punk Anderson
6. Vaughn Leland
7. Jordan Lee
8. Gary Ewing
9. Harv Smithfield
10. Harrison Page

Robbing the Cradle

Quiz 34
1979—80 Season

1. What did J. R. and Sue Ellen name their son?
2. Where was he kidnapped?
3. Who was Mrs. Reeves?
4. Whom did Pam first suspect had kidnapped her nephew?
5. Who were the two phony kidnappers? Where had they just come from?
6. How much ransom did the phony kidnappers demand?
7. Where did they tell J. R. that he'd find his son?
8. Who had really taken John Ross?
9. Where had Pam seen the kidnapper?
10. What was the real kidnapper's motive?

There's No Resistin' Kristin

Quiz 35
1979—80 Season

1. What family event brought Kristin back to Dallas?
2. Who called Kristin "Lady Dracula"?
3. How did Kristin address Sue Ellen's father-in-law?
4. Who was Lanny Markward?
5. What job did Kristin take at Ewing Oil? Whom did she replace?
6. How did Mrs. Shepard feel about Kristin pursuing J. R.? Why?
7. What was the Oakside condominium?
8. Who told Kristin: "With your kind of mind and your kind of body, it might take me a lifetime to fully appreciate you"?
9. What young banker in Santa Fe was Kristin's ex-boyfriend?
10. Who became Kristin's partner in crime?

Digger's Disease

Quiz 36
1979—80 Season

1. What is the medical term for Digger Barnes's disease?
2. How does it affect the body?
3. Is it fatal?
4. How is it transmitted?
5. Who were Tyler and Catherine?
6. Is there a cure for Digger's disease?
7. Why was Pam afraid to tell Bobby about it?
8. Why was Pam afraid to tell Sue Ellen about it?
9. Does John Ross have it?
10. Is Pam herself a carrier? Why?

Traps and Triumphs

Quiz 37
1979—80 Season

1. In what part of the world did J. R. buy a very expensive group of oil leases?
2. Who was his banker?
3. What did J. R. have to mortgage in order to get the bank to arrange financial backing for his foreign oil scheme?
4. What was Lucy's favorite extracurricular activity during her first year of college?
5. Whose business philosophy was "If you can't beat up the other guy you verbally twist him like a pretzel"?
6. How long were Jock and Amanda Lewis married?
7. What happened to Amanda Lewis?
8. What prompted Jock to reveal the secret of his first marriage?
9. Bobby once said, "Take Tahiti, not the living room furniture." Whom was he advising—and what was his logic?
10. Sue Ellen once called someone in her life her "punishment" from God. Who?

Missing Places

1. Jock was shot by a sniper while on a hunting trip in _____.
2. The Southern Cross ranch was located in _____.
3. Alan Beam had grown up in the midwestern city of _____.
4. Dusty and Sue Ellen met secretly at the Regent Hotel in _____.
5. Jenna Wade's daughter, Charlie, frequently visited her father in _____.
6. Dusty fantasized about marrying Sue Ellen and honeymooning in _____.
7. Jock and Ellie visited Amanda Ewing at her sanitarium in _____.
8. In order to spend the night with Dusty, Sue Ellen told Miss Ellie she was flying to _____ to visit her sorority sister.
9. Pam spent her earliest childhood years in the Texas city of _____.
10. If Cliff Barnes had won his campaign he would have gone to _____.

Dusty and Sue Ellen

Quiz 39
1979—80 Season

1. What was Dusty's real name?
2. What brought him to Dallas?
3. When Dusty bumped into Sue Ellen at Hector's Place, what was the first thing he did?
4. What was Hector's Place?
5. What special meaning did the numbers 721, 1701, and 23 have?
6. Why was Sue Ellen afraid to divorce J. R.?
7. How did Sue Ellen learn of Dusty's death?
8. Where was she at the time?
9. What was the first thing she did?
10. How did Dusty die?

Friends and Enemies

Match the characters in Column A with the descriptions that fit them best in Column B.

Column A
1. Matt Devlin
2. Hank Johnson
3. Deborah Johns
4. Barry Lester
5. Jonas Smithers
6. Mary Lou Hensley
7. Linda Bradley
8. Scotty Demerest
9. Hutch McKinney
10. Tom Miller

Column B
a. Sam and Donna's attorney
b. corpse buried on South-fork.
c. snoopy *Dallas Press* reporter
d. Sue Ellen's college chum
e. condo builder of Mimosa Park
f. Sue Ellen hired him to spy on J. R.
g. J. R.'s representative in Asia
h. Cliff's law school buddy
i. Marilee's shadow
j. Jock's defense attorney at his murder trial

Missing Persons

Quiz 41
1979—80 Season

1. Dr. Ellby's first name was _____.
2. _____ ,an anthropology professor, helped solve the _____ murder mystery.
3. Lyle Sloan worked with _____ in the district attorney's office.
4. Luke's father _____ was bitten by a rattlesnake.
5. Miss Ellie's adversary turned not-so-secret admirer was _____.
6. _____ spilled a drink on Sue Ellen's dress to convince everyone that Sue Ellen was off the wagon.
7. _____ had a miscarriage when she was thrown from a horse.
8. _____, _____, and Sue Ellen all took blood tests to determine John Ross's paternity.
9. When the Ewings visited Amanda at the sanitarium, she mistook _____ for Jock,
10. The man who shot Hutch McKinney turned out to be _____.

Forgotten Facts

Quiz 42
1979–80 Season

1. Why did Donna reconcile with Sam Culver?
2. Who was fashion editor of *Elite* magazine?
3. Where did Lucy meet Alan Beam?
4. Who was Luanne Culver?
5. Where did Bobby run into Jenna Wade after an eighteen-month absence?
6. When Lucy developed a sudden interest in her literature course, what book did she become absolutely engrossed in?
7. What Dallas park did Miss Ellie and the Daughters of the Alamo fight to preserve?
8. Whom did J. R. employ to sabotage Cliff Barnes's campaign?
9. Who made Kristin's eyes light up when she heard he was worth $40 million?
10. Who was Betty Lou Barker?

Vital Title Statistics

Quiz 43
1979—80 Season

1. The episode dealing with Digger's disease was called:
   a. "Digger's Disease";
   b. "The Silent Killer";
   c. "Pam's Anguish."
2. Jock's near fatal hunting expedition was titled:
   a. "The Dove Hunt";
   b. "Survival";
   c. "The Sniper's Bullet."
3. Sue Ellen met Dusty in the episode called:
   a. "Bronco";
   b. "Rodeo";
   c. "Sue Ellen's Reawakening."
4. "The Heiress" dealt with the romance between:
   a. Sue Ellen and Dusty;
   b. Alan and Lucy;
   c. Ray and Donna.
5. "Return Engagement" focused on the reuniting of:
   a. Bobby and Pam;
   b. J. R. and Kristin;
   c. Gary and Val.
6. "Sue Ellen's Choice" dealt with her ambivalent feelings about:
   a. sex;
   b. motherhood;
   c. divorce.

7. The two-part show about the kidnapping of J. R.'s son was called:
   a. "Kidnapped";
   b. "The Lost Child";
   c. "Whatever Happened to Baby John?"
8. "Ellie Saves the Day" dealt with Miss Ellie's success in:
   a. stopping Sue Ellen and J. R.'s divorce;
   b. preventing Lucy from marrying Alan Beam;
   c. unmortgaging Southfork.
9. Pam learned that Digger Barnes wasn't her real father in the episode called:
   a. "The Silent Killer";
   b. "Jock's Trial";
   c. "Secrets."
10. J. R. was shot in the last show of the season. It was titled:
    a. "Who Shot J.R.?";
    b. "End of the Road";
    c. "A House Divided."

The Shot Heard 'Round the World

Quiz 44
1979—80 Season

Who made each of the following threats, comments, and observations just before J. R. was shot?

1. "I have to get as far away from J. R. as possible."
2. "I'll see to it that this is the last crooked deal you ever pull."
3. "I'm sorry, Daddy . . . J. R. whipped me."
4. "He has to be stopped. He'll teach my son to be like him."
5. "J. R. did right. . . . I would have done the same myself."
6. "I don't appreciate being treated like some clerk."
7. "You're a dead man, J. R."
8. "You knew those wells were . . . worthless—you suckered your friends into buying the leases."
9. "You know I don't want Bobby to leave. You know that."
10. "I'll kill him. I swear I'll kill him."

Wild, Wild Guests

Quiz 45
1980—81 Season

Do you remember these guest stars and regulars who joined the show during the 1980—81 season? Name the actor or actress who created each unforgettable role.

1. Mitch Cooper
2. Afton Cooper
3. Amos Krebbs
4. Rebecca Wentworth
5. Arliss Cooper
6. Leslie Stewart
7. Clint Ogden
8. Alex Ward
9. Marilee Stone
10. Craig Stewart

Who Shot J.R.? ...
The Morning After

1. Who discovered J. R.'s body? Where?
2. J. R. had been shot twice. What injuries did each of those bullets cause?
3. Who was Cy Frost?
4. Who was Carl Roclaire?
5. Who said "If J. R. was dead, I couldn't mourn him"?
6. Where was Lucy when J. R. was shot?
7. Who mistakenly believed that she had tried to murder J. R.?
8. J. R. was operated on to remove what internal organ?
9. Who kept a constant vigil with Sue Ellen at the hospital?
10. Where was Cliff Barnes around the time of the shooting?
11. Which suspect had just checked into a Missouri motel when the shooting occurred?
12. Which suspect was in his lawyer's office when the murder attempt took place? What was he doing there?
13. After the shooting who found J. R.'s gun? Where? What was significant about it?
14. Who had recurring nightmares about the shooting?
15. After Cliff's release who became the prime suspect?

Who Shot J.R.? . . .
The Suspects

Quiz 47
1980—81 Season

What motive did each of these characters have for wanting to murder ''Texas's answer to Michael Corleone''?

1. Alan Beam
2. Sue Ellen Ewing
3. Cliff Barnes
4. Marilee Stone
5. Vaughn Leland
6. Kristin Shepard
7. Valene Ewing
8. Pamela Ewing
9. Jordan Lee
10. Miss Ellie

Who Shot J. R.? . . .
Sue Ellen's Ordeal

Quiz 48
1980—81 Season

1. What was the most incriminating, tangible piece of evidence against Sue Ellen?
2. Who was her attorney?
3. Who persuaded him that defending Sue Ellen might be a costly mistake?
4. After her arraignment how much bail was set?
5. Who did Sue Ellen mistakenly think had put up her bail money?
6. Where did Sue Ellen go first after her release from jail?
7. She begged Bobby to do her one favor. What was it?
8. Since Sue Ellen couldn't return to Southfork, where did she take up residence?
9. Where did Sue Ellen enjoy a brief visit with John Ross?
10. Who brought John Ross to that prearranged meeting place?

Who Shot J.R.? ...
The Moment of Truth

1. What couldn't Sue Ellen remember?
2. How did Dr. Ellby jog her memory?
3. On the day J. R. was shot, after putting the gun in her purse, where had Sue Ellen gone?
4. What was her next stop?
5. What was her third stop?
6. Where did she leave the gun?
7. What had Sue Ellen been looking for in Kristin's apartment?
8. What had Kristin given her?
9. Where did Sue Ellen wake up the next morning?
10. When she got back to Southfork, who told her that J. R. had been shot?

Who Shot J. R? . . .
A Little More Target Practice

Quiz 50
1980—81 Season

1. In a special poll whom did the readers of *People* magazine pick as the person most likely to have pulled the trigger on J. R.?
2. On what date was the real culprit revealed to *Dallas* viewers?
3. The denouement was supposed to air in early October. Why was the suspense prolonged for an extra seven weeks?
4. What did Lee Rich, Philip Capice, Leonard Katzman, Arthur Bernard Lewis, and Camille Marchetta have in common?
5. During the summer of 1980, a J. R. bumper sticker became extremely popular. What did it say?
6. Whom did English bookmakers rate as a 14–1 longshot as the would-be assassin?
7. What contribution did a Yamaha CS-80 synthesizer make to the who-shot-J. R. story?
8. What Republican presidential candidate had an airtight alibi: he was getting killed in the New Hampshire primary that day?
9. Who did Larry Hagman jokingly suggest had shot J. R.?
10. By the way, who *did* shoot J. R.?

Lucy and Mitch

Quiz 51
1980—81 Season

1. What was Mitch Cooper's job at The Time Warp Club?
2. What was he studying to be?
3. How did Mitch ask Lucy to marry him?
4. Whose dress did Lucy wear on her wedding day?
5. What was Jock's wedding gift to Mitch and Lucy?
6. What job did J. R. offer Mitch?
7. What old acquaintance did Sue Ellen run into at Lucy's wedding reception?
8. What did Val and Gary give Lucy on her wedding day?
9. Every bride wears something borrowed. What did Pam loan Lucy?
10. As for something blue, what did Sue Ellen find for Lucy?

A Few More Twisters

Quiz 52
1980—81 Season

1. What unusual paraphernalia did Mitch Cooper bring along on his honeymoon?
2. While J. R. was recovering from his gunshot wounds, who ran Ewing Oil?
3. As a baby what was John Ross called by the rest of the family?
4. An oil man named Justin Carlisle was responsible for introducing the Ewings to a very high-powered blonde. Who was she?
5. What was her profession?
6. What did Clint Ogden's company manufacture?
7. What did Jock, Ray, and Punk Anderson want to build in the Takapa wilderness?
8. Why did Sue Ellen say that she and Pam both shared the "Ewing disease"?
9. Who did J. R. tell, "I like a woman whose taste runs a little to the bizarre at times"? Why? Where were they?
10. Why did Sue Ellen buy a brand-new bed and mattress right after Lucy's wedding?
11. Who became interested in solar energy?
12. Who wanted to start a revolution? Where?

A Touch of Romance

1. Pam and Alex Ward mixed business with pleasure at the Gulf resort of _____.
2. _____ and _____ reminisced about their first date at the Starlight Roof of the Grandview Hotel.
3. Without Mitch's knowledge Lucy hired a _____.
4. Appleton was a _____, hired by _____ to follow Sue Ellen.
5. Cliff thought _____ would back him to replace Dave Culver as state senator.
6. _____'s extended business trip to Oklahoma City nearly cost him his marriage.
7. _____ helped Afton get her first singing job in Dallas.
8. When Leslie Stewart turned down J. R.'s advances, he spent the night with his old flame, _____.
9. Mitch was distressed when Lucy became _____.
10. When Bobby won the state senate race, Pam's gift to him was an old-fashioned _____.

Feminine Mystique

Quiz 54
1980—81 Season

Match the ladies in Column A with the descriptions that fit them best in Column B.

Column A
1. Dolores
2. Jean
3. Alicia
4. Jackie
5. Arliss
6. Rebecca
7. Margaret
8. Leslie
9. Sally
10. Kristin

Column B
a. "People Before Profits"
b. J. R. sent her to the Bahamas
c. Lucy's cleaning woman
d. the mother of J. R.'s other son?
e. Eugene Bullock's better half
f. Hunter was her maiden name
g. Mitch's medical school pal
h. she saw Pam with Alex Ward
i. Bobby liked her veal marsala
j. Sue Ellen couldn't break up her marriage

More Doings with the Ewings

Quiz 55
1980—81 Season

1. Who was born on October 19, 1945?
2. What event prompted Rebecca's permanent return to Dallas?
3. Who said, "The ball's in your court now, J. R."? What was meant by that remark?
4. What financial arrangement did Jock make upon learning that Ray was his natural son?
5. Who celebrated the end of their bitter battle with a second honeymoon?
6. Who gave Bobby an egg salad on white sandwich and some good advice?
7. Who did Sue Ellen find on Denton Street?
8. Who got up in the middle of the night to wash dishes? Why?
9. Where had Jock met Ray Krebbs's mother?
10. What was Cliff's initial reaction to Rebecca's reappearance in Dallas?
11. Why did Miss Ellie consult a lawyer named Lincoln Hargrave?
12. How did Bobby's compromise solve the battle over the Takapa wilderness preserve?

Name That Show!

Match the episode titles in Column A with the appropriate descriptions in Column B.

Column A
1. "Who Done It?"
2. "The Fourth Son"
3. "The Prodigal Mother"
4. "The New Mrs. Ewing"
5. "Ewing vs. Ewing"
6. "Nightmare"
7. "Start the Revolution with Me"
8. "Ewing-gate"
9. "Executive Wife"
10. "No More Mr. Nice Guy"

Column B
a. Pam finds Rebecca Wentworth
b. the cleaning woman finds J. R.
c. Kristin takes the final plunge
d. Sue Ellen undergoes hypnosis
e. while Pam minds the Store, who's minding Pam?
f. Donna joins the clan
g. J. R. tries a new ploy in Asia
h. Miss Ellie considers divorcing Jock
i. Amos Krebbs comes to visit Ray
j. Sue Ellen decides she must have shot J. R.

Wild, Wild Guests

Quiz 57
1981—82 Season

Another crop of talented arrivals rang the bell at Ewing Oil as *Dallas* entered its fourth season on network television. Please identify the actor or actress who made each of these characters famous.

1. Katherine Wentworth
2. Dr. Frank Waring
3. Jeff Farraday
4. Evelyn Michaelson
5. Roger Larson
6. Dee Dee Webster
7. Bonnie Robertson
8. Blair Sullivan
9. Arthur Elrod
10. Dr. Dagmara Conrad

Splashy Ending

1. Where was Kristin's body discovered?
2. How did she happen to land there?
3. Who was accused of murdering her?
4. What did a lie detector test prove?
5. Who was Emmett Walsh?
6. What two substances were found in Kristin's body?
7. What was the verdict at the coroner's inquest?
8. Who brought Sue Ellen the news of Kristin's death?
9. Where was Sue Ellen at the time?
10. Where was Kristin buried?

The Bitter and the Sweet

Quiz 59
1981—82 Season

1. What was Jock's favorite dish?
2. In what county was the Southern Cross located?
3. Who delivered John Ross to Sue Ellen when she moved to the Southern Cross?
4. What did J. R. do in his son's empty nursery?
5. Who became president of Wentworth Tool and Die?
6. What did Clark Crandall offer Bobby?
7. Who made Cliff's favorite dessert (chocolate pie) for him?
8. What did Mitch do to Dr. Waring's wife?
9. Who was Milton?
10. Who was Fred?

Custody Battle

Quiz 60
1981–82 Season

1. Where was the first place J. R. tried to snatch back his son from Sue Ellen and Dusty?
2. Who ordered J. R. to bring the boy back to Southfork?
3. How did Miss Ellie go to the Southern Cross to visit John Ross?
4. What did J. R. beg her to do on that occasion? What was her response?
5. Who was Arthur Elrod?
6. How did J. R. expect to prove Sue Ellen an unfit mother?
7. Why did Dusty's impotency help Sue Ellen's case?
8. Whose side did Miss Ellie take in the custody case?
9. Who won temporary custody of John Ross?
10. What was J. R.'s final scheme to get his son back?
11. Who was awarded final custody of John Ross?
12. What was Sue Ellen's alimony settlement?

Loaded with Blanks

1. Dr. Waring's medical specialty was _____.
2. Bobby rescued a distraught Pam from the top of _____.
3. Pam was admitted as a patient at _____ Psychiatric Hospital.
4. As a doctor Mitch originally wanted to specialize in _____.
5. Pam was diagnosed as suffering from severe _____.
6. While Sue Ellen chatted with Clayton, Dusty spent every night in the Southern Cross _____.
7. The U.S. government sent Jock down to _____ to help develop new sources of _____.
8. Bobby paid _____ to _____ for a copy of Christopher's _____.
9. While Pam was in the sanitarium, _____ and _____ decided to redecorate her bedroom.
10. In New York Katherine Wentworth was trying to build a career as a _____.

Counselors, Cohorts, and Con Men

Quiz 62
1981–82 Season

Match the characters in Column A with the descriptions that fit them best in Column B.

Column A
1. Edward Chapman
2. Walter Sherr
3. Jordan Lee
4. Billy Bob McCoy
5. Howard Barker
6. Vaughn Leland
7. Wally Hampton
8. Charles Eccles
9. Henry Webster
10. Paul Winslow

Column B
a. J. R. wanted Afton to sleep with him
b. Donna's publisher
c. J. R.'s New York stock-broker
d. offered Cliff a phony out-of-state job
e. Ray's business partner
f. sent Kristin a whopper of a check
g. Sue Ellen's divorce decree turned him on
h. oil broker
i. advised Bobby on Christopher's adoption
j. J. R.'s lawyer at final custody hearing

Courageous Women . . .
Outrageous Ladies

Quiz 63
1981–82 Season

Match the characters in Column A with the descriptions that fit them best in Column B.

Column A
1. Beverly Waring
2. Miss Ellie
3. Dagmara Conrad
4. Evelyn Michaelson
5. Liz Craig
6. Geraldine Crane
7. Caroline Carter
8. Sly Lovegren
9. Bonnie Robertson
10. Katherine Wentworth

Column B
a. she loaned Ray $1,000,000
b. Mitch's lonely tennis partner
c. Lucy and Mitch went to her party—separately
d. Bobby bought her aerobics salon
e. she called Cliff a "disgusting little man"
f. Pam's psychiatrist
g. she called McSween "Uncle Harry"
h. she told Bobby to find work for Pam
i. representative from Smithfield and Bennett
j. Ray hugged her—and Donna slugged her

Share and Share Alike

Quiz 64
1981–82 Season

Shortly before his death Jock sent Miss Ellie a fateful letter from South America. In that letter he divided up Ewing Oil stock among his family, so that the business would continue to run smoothly in his absence. How many voting shares were each of these family members given?

1. Miss Ellie
2. J. R.
3. Bobby
4. Sue Ellen
5. Pam
6. Gary
7. Ray
8. Lucy
9. John Ross III
10. Christopher

That Fateful Barbecue

Quiz 65
1981—82 Season

1. Larry Deltham was Miss Ellie's _____.
2. Miss Ellie threw the barbecue to celebrate _____'s impending return from _____.
3. At the party everyone was congratulating Donna on the publication of her book, _____.
4. While Pam stayed with Christopher, Bobby danced with _____.
5. Another surprise dance couple were Clayton and _____.
6. Miss Ellie made J. R. very happy by arranging for _____ to be at the festivities.
7. Miss Ellie and Rebecca were hoping the barbecue would be a step toward ending the _____.
8. Lucy's dance partner at the barbecue was _____.
9. The day ended in tragedy when Miss Ellie got a call from _____.
10. He told her that Jock had been lost in a _____.

The Search for Jock

Quiz 66
1981–82 Season

1. Which three members of the clan flew down to South America to search for Jock?
2. Who wanted to go with them but was finally convinced not to?
3. Who did Miss Ellie put in charge of the search mission?
4. What did Miss Ellie ask Sue Ellen to do?
5. Who dove into the lake where Jock's helicopter had crashed?
6. What did he find?
7. While the search went on, who thought back to the time of Jock's bypass surgery?
8. Who recalled how happy Jock had been when she'd announced her pregnancy?
9. Whose memories focused on a hospital waiting room and the birth of a child?
10. What happened on the porch of Southfork after the rescue mission returned from South America?

Close Calls and Cliff-Hangers

Quiz 67
1981—82 Season

1. What gift did Clayton buy for Sue Ellen that he never gave her?
2. In what city did Bobby find out the truth about Christopher's parentage?
3. What happened to the child that Kristin had conceived by J. R.?
4. What oil field turned out to be Cliff's Waterloo?
5. What woman helped J. R. dupe Cliff into buying the wrong oil field?
6. How did Cliff try to kill himself?
7. Who found Cliff unconscious and phoned for help?
8. Who announced, ''The Barnes-Ewing feud is still going on. . . . I swear I'll break the Ewing family . . . and I have the money to do it.''
9. What did Miss Ellie do when she found out about Cliff's suicide attempt?
10. If Cliff died what did Sue Ellen say she wouldn't be able to do?

Good News and Bad

Quiz 68
1981–82 Season

1. Who was born on August 18, 1981?
2. Who did Clayton remind Sue Ellen of?
3. Where would you expect to find Inga?
4. Who lived at 960 Bowie Street?
5. What city did Sue Ellen represent at the Miss Texas beauty pageant?
6. Who found whom at the Starbright Motel?
7. What is the name of Marilee's company?
8. What did Jerry Macon do for J. R.?
9. What made Lucy become frightened of Roger?
10. What did Bobby find in apartment 212?

Wild, Wild Guests

Quiz 69
1982—83 Season

Dallas welcomed several new faces during the 1982—83 season. Can you supply the actor or actress who created each of these roles?

1. Lil Trotter
2. Frank Crutcher
3. Walt Driscoll
4. Holly Harwood
5. Mark Graison
6. Brooks Oliver
7. Mickey Trotter
8. George Hicks
9. Gil Thurman
10. Roy Ralston

Bedside Brainteasers

Quiz 70
1982—83 Season

1. Where did Cliff recover from his suicide attempt?
2. While Cliff lingered between life and death, what did Sue Ellen regret the most?
3. Who told Sue Ellen to stay out of Cliff's life because "you're poison"?
4. What did J. R. do at Sue Ellen's town house while she kept a vigil at the hospital?
5. Why did the doctors worry that Cliff might emerge from his coma brain-damaged?
6. Who was with Cliff when he regained consciousness?
7. Who did he ask for?
8. What was he really suffering from once he woke up?
9. What forceful visitor helped change Cliff's bleak attitude?
10. Who told Afton, "I hope you and Cliff can make it together and find happiness"?

Just Asking . . .

Quiz 71
1982–83 Season

1. How did Holly Harwood become president of her own oil company?
2. What share of ownership did Holly give J. R.?
3. Who were Ted Pendergast and Rick Miller?
4. In the family vote to remove J. R. as head of Ewing Oil, what was the outcome?
5. Who voted to remove J. R. as president?
6. Who voted to keep J. R. as president?
7. Why couldn't Miss Ellie vote John Ross's shares?
8. Why couldn't Ray vote?
9. Who took over as head of Ewing oil?
10. What did J. R. stay home and do after he lost his job?

Men with a Mission

Quiz 72
1982–83 Season

Match the gentlemen in Column A with the descriptions that fit them best in Column B.

Column A
1. Brooks Oliver
2. Mark Graison
3. Walt Driscoll
4. John Baxter
5. Punk Anderson
6. Mitch Cooper
7. Frank Crutcher
8. Mickey Trotter
9. Dave Culver
10. Eugene Bullock

Column B
a. Bobby valued his oil tankers—and his advice
b. Lucy caught him checking out the family silver
c. he didn't bother to contest the divorce
d. Mark Graison's attorney
e. he offered Donna a seat on the Texas Energy Commission
f. his kindness to Miss Ellie charmed Pam
g. the administrator of Jock's will
h. he wanted Miss Ellie to join him in New York
i. he helped J. R. get a sneak peek at the will
j. J. R. got his oil variance thanks to this frightened friend

The Second Time Around

Quiz 73
1982—83 Season

1. Who gave the bride away at Sue Ellen's remarriage to J.R.?
2. Who was matron of honor?
3. Who was best man?
4. Who personally invited Cliff to the wedding?
5. Who was Cliff's guest?
6. Who nearly interrupted the wedding ceremony?
7. Why didn't Lucy attend the wedding?
8. At the wedding reception who disinvited Cliff? Why?
9. What did Cliff do that angered J. R.?
10. What did Clayton, Cliff, J. R., Bobby, and Ray all do at the reception?
11. Who left the wedding with an injured wrist?
12. Who left with a bruised jaw?
13. Why did Mike Sidney show up at J. R. and Sue Ellen's honeymoon cottage?
14. What unusual sights did Sue Ellen get to see on her second honeymoon?
15. Of her two honeymoons, which did she rate as more "interesting"?

Brothers at War

Quiz 74
1982–83 Season

1. Why was Lee Evans a key witness at the hearing to declare Jock legally dead?
2. According to Jock's will, what did Miss Ellie inherit?
3. What financial provisions did Jock make for Ray and Gary?
4. Was the codicil regarding control of Ewing Oil typed or handwritten? Who witnessed it?
5. The codicil set up a contest between Bobby and J. R. For how long? How would the company be split during that time?
6. When the contest ended, what would the winner receive?
7. What would the loser receive?
8. How would the remaining shares of Ewing Oil be divided?
9. What did Lucy receive in her grandfather's will?
10. If the court had not declared Jock legally dead, what would have happened?

Maverick Mementos

Quiz 75
1982—83 Season

1. Of all Jock's belongings, what did Miss Ellie have the most trouble giving away?
2. What happened on November 24, 1982?
3. Which four people attended Amos Krebbs's funeral?
4. What chore did Ray do for Aunt Lil when he visited her in Kansas?
5. Who never got to go dancing at the Rainbow Room?
6. What did Mickey call the bunkhouse at Southfork the first time he saw it?
7. Walt Driscoll's wife was arrested three times. On what charge?
8. Why did Pam surp.ise Bobby with balloons, streamers, and champagne in their bedroom?
9. Who did Jock think was a stronger person—Lucy or Gary?
10. Who liked pistachio ice cream?

Scrambled Scripts

Quiz 76
1982–83 Season

Column A lists ten script titles from the 1982–83 season. Match each title with the appropriate plot synopsis in Column B.

Column A
1. "Hit and Run"
2. "Ewing Inferno"
3. "Mama Dearest"
4. "Fringe Benefits"
5. "Crash of '83"
6. "The Sting"
7. "Tangled Web"
8. "The Big Ball"
9. "Post-Nuptial"
10. "Cuba-Libre"

Column B
a. Miss Ellie stops mourning for Jock
b. J. R. visits a foreign jail
c. Cliff and J. R. come to blows
d. J. R. sets up Walt Driscoll for blackmail
e. Sue Ellen fends off Gil Thurman
f. Miss Ellie considers court action to overturn Jock's will
g. Ray's brawl with J. R. leads to tragedy
h. Sue Ellen catches Holly Harwood in a compromising situation
i. Rebecca changes places with Cliff
j. Ray and Bobby team up to stop Walt Driscoll

The Tension Builds

Quiz 77
1982–83 Season

1. Who called Lucy a "block of ice"?
2. Who were Henry Figueroa, Elmer Lawrence, and Doug Reed?
3. How did Pam and Sue Ellen decide to handle the war between their husbands?
4. Who set up a dummy corporation called Petro/State?
5. Who was the leader of the mob scene at Miss Ellie's barbecue?
6. Who were they threatening?
7. As a result of that mob scene, what two things did Miss Ellie threaten to do?
8. What is Miss Ellie's favorite midnight snack?
9. According to Donna, what's the one disadvantage of being married to a cowboy?
10. What was the cause of Lucy's despondency?
11. What did Mrs. Rafferty, the real estate agent, call Afton?
12. Was Brooks Oliver considerably younger or considerably older than Miss Ellie?
13. What was Holly Harwood's favorite business attire?
14. Who told the press, "There is only one Ewing who really cares about the little man"?
15. What was the name of Roy Ralston's TV show?

Miss Ellie Goes to Court

Quiz 78
1982–83 Season

1. On what legal grounds did Miss Ellie contest Jock's will?
2. What family member was most supportive of Miss Ellie's decision?
3. What two family members were most staunchly against her?
4. What was Sue Ellen's position?
5. Why did Harv Smithfield disqualify himself as Miss Ellie's attorney?
6. Who recommended Brooks Oliver to Miss Ellie?
7. If Jock's new will was overturned in favor of his old one, what two family members would be disinherited?
8. What U.S. senator testified at the hearing? What did he call Jock's trip to South America?
9. What physical condition was Jock suffering from at the time he wrote the codicil?
10. What was the judge's verdict?

The Suspense Is Intense

Quiz 79
1982—83 Season

1. Why was General Cochran angry at J. R.?
2. What did Bobby get from Carl Daggett?
3. Who asked Pam if Christopher was going to throw up on him?
4. Why did Lucy let Mickey drive her to the airport?
5. Who brought Pam the news of her mother's plane crash?
6. On her deathbed what promise did Rebecca exact from Pam?
7. Whose vote on the Texas Energy Commission was decisive in revoking J. R.'s oil variance?
8. Did J. R. attend Rebecca Wentworth's funeral?
9. Who did Bobby see having lunch together at the Summerhill restaurant? Who had planned the whole encounter?
10. Who negotiated J. R.'s Cuban oil deal?

Southfork in Flames!

Quiz 80
1982–83 Season

1. What made Sue Ellen start drinking again?
2. When Sue Ellen threw a bottle of wine at J. R., where did it land?
3. Why was Ray enraged at J. R.?
4. Why did J. R. call Clouse Interior Decorators? What did they bring to Southfork?
5. What became of Walt Driscoll?
6. How did the fire at Southfork actually start?
7. What two people were asleep in the house at the time?
8. Why was Sue Ellen in a particularly deep sleep?
9. Where was Miss Ellie?
10. Whose arrival home just in the nick of time saved everyone's lives?

Wild, Wild Guests

Quiz 81
1983—84 Season

A number of illustrious guest stars passed through the gates of Southfork during the 1983–84 season. What actor or actress created each of these memorable roles?

1. Peter Richards
2. Jessica Montford
3. Edgar Randolph
4. Martha Randolph
5. Paul Morgan
6. Renaldo Marchetta
7. Harry McSween
8. Jenna Wade
9. Charlie Wade
10. Percy McManus

Landmarks for Lovers

Quiz 82
1983—84 Season

1. Where did Bobby meet Jenna Wade after a four-year absence? What was she doing there?
2. Where did Clayton and Miss Ellie honeymoon?
3. At what hotel did J. R. and Sue Ellen reside after the Southfork fire?
4. What arena did Mark jestingly recommend to Pam as a wedding site?
5. After his trial ended where did Ray take Donna for a second honeymoon?
6. What did Bobby and Pam do when they met in Thanksgiving Square?
7. In what city did Cliff's secret tryst with Marilee take place? And where was Afton at the time?
8. What pair of lovers met furtively at McNaughton's Point?
9. Where is Jenna's ex-husband now? Who paid him a surprise visit there?
10. What couple were in Jamaica during Ray's murder trial?

Bobby and Jenna

Quiz 83
1983—84 Season

1. How did Bobby become Jenna's landlord?
2. How old is Jenna's daughter Charlie?
3. Does Jenna own or rent her town house?
4. What is Jenna's ex-husband's nationality? What is his title?
5. How does J. R. feel about Bobby's romance with Jenna?
6. What remark of Jenna's prompted Pam to leave Dallas?
7. On her first date with Bobby why did Jenna order dessert even though she wasn't hungry?
8. How did Jenna infuriate Pam at the Good Old Boys' Charity Rodeo?
9. What happened to Jenna's family inheritance?
10. How did Katherine Wentworth nearly discredit Jenna in Bobby's eyes?

Pam and Mark

Quiz 84
1983—84 Season

1. What prompted Mark to tell Christopher, "The plans your mother and I had may have just gone up in smoke"?
2. Who was Tracy Anders?
3. What was Mark's private wager with Tracy?
4. Mark's fatal illness began innocently enough with a simple knee injury. How did it happen?
5. How did Mark feel about Cliff's offshore oil venture?
6. What was Mark's favorite sport?
7. What was the name of his oil company?
8. Who told Pam that Mark was dying?
9. How did Mark end his life?
10. What did Fred Robinson later bring Pam?

Clayton and Miss Ellie

Quiz 85
1983—84 Season

1. What was Miss Ellie's biggest fear about marrying Clayton?
2. What was the name of Clayton's first wife?
3. Who were Dusty's real parents?
4. Who invited Jessica to Southfork?
5. Who became Jessica's ally in trying to stop the wedding?
6. On the day Jessica went crazy where were she and Miss Ellie supposedly going? Who was with them?
7. What gave J. R. the idea that his mother was in danger?
8. Who burned down the Southern Cross?
9. Who finally disarmed Jessica and rescued Miss Ellie?
10. Who was matron of honor at Clayton and Miss Ellie's wedding? Who was best man?

Sue Ellen and Peter

Quiz 86
1983—84 Season

1. How did Sue Ellen meet Peter Richards?
2. What subject was he majoring in at college?
3. Why did he take an apartment off campus?
4. Was he the father of the baby that Sue Ellen miscarried?
5. Who was Jerry Hunter?
6. Who had Peter arrested on a phony drug rap?
7. Where were the drugs found?
8. On what condition did J. R. offer to get the drug charge against Peter dropped?
9. What was Sue Ellen's reaction?
10. What was Peter's reaction?

Who Pulled the Plug on Mickey?

Quiz 87
1983—84 Season

1. How did Mickey Trotter actually die?
2. Besides Ray, who was the only other person in Mickey's hospital room when death occurred?
3. What attorney defended Ray?
4. Who was the prosecuting attorney?
5. Did Ray testify on his own behalf?
6. Was Lucy a witness for the prosecution or the defense?
7. Mickey become paralyzed as the result of a car accident. Who was in the car with him? Who was driving the other car?
8. Whom did everyone hold indirectly responsible for Mickey's accident? Why?
9. Whom did J. R. blame?
10. At the pretrial arraignment how much bail was set?
11. Why didn't Harv Smithfield personally handle Ray's defense?
12. Did Lucy approve of what Ray had done?
13. Did Donna?
14. Did Aunt Lil?
15. What was Ray's sentence?

The Oil Barons' Ball

Quiz 88
1983—84 Season

1. Who was the chairman of the ball?
2. Who was Pam's date? Who was Bobby's date?
3. Who was voted Oil Man of the Year?
4. For what achievement?
5. What man did the winner praise in his acceptance speech? What man did he vilify?
6. Why were Frank Warren, Sherrill Lynne, Mitchell Wayne, and Kevin Christopher at the ball?
7. Who was Lucy's escort for the evening?
8. What five women had a fiery meeting in the powder room?
9. Who announced the establishment of the Digger Barnes Scholarship?
10. To where did J. R. say the winner should be sent?
11. Whose formal attire was generously paid for by J. R.?
12. Who got hit with a tray full of desserts?
13. Why was Katherine furious?
14. Who was master of ceremonies that night?
15. Who bit J. R.?

Famous Firsts

True, we only know these ladies on a first-name basis and rarely give them a second glance, but each has become an inimitable fixture on *Dallas*. See how many you can recognize by matching each lady in Column A with the description that best fits her in Column B.

Column A
1. Dora Mae
2. Sly
3. Phyllis
4. Teresa
5. Muriel
6. Kendall
7. Serena
8. Jackie
9. Louise
10. Caroline

Column B
a. J. R.'s favorite call girl
b. counselor at John Ross's camp
c. keeps Southfork running smoothly
d. Ewing Oil receptionist
e. Pam's housekeeper
f. hostess at the Oil Barons' Club
g. Bobby's secretary
h. dictation whiz/double agent
i. Lucy's best friend
j. "Hello, Barnes/Wentworth"

Hangouts and Hideouts

Quiz 90
1983—84 Season

How many of these *Dallas* weigh stations and watering holes can you name?

1. J. R. and Harry McSween's favorite burger joint
2. Sue Ellen and Mickey Trotter were both patients there.
3. Jessica's current address
4. John Ross's day camp
5. Sue Ellen loved the dresses—and the champagne!
6. Jessica held Miss Ellie hostage in this motel.
7. site of the annual Good Old Boys' Charity Rodeo
8. where Peter Richards attends classes
9. it's meals-and-deals-on-wheels for J. R. here
10. the section of Southfork where Ray, Bobby, and J. R. held a memorable summit meeting about Mickey's accident

Strictly Professional

Match each character in Column A with the proper identifying tag in Column B.

Column A
1. Jerry Kenderson
2. Travis Boyd
3. Max Flowers
4. Andy Bradley
5. Leo Wakefield
6. Ben Kesey
7. Toni Jeffries
8. Ed Hoffman
9. Suzanne Lacey
10. Armando Sidoni
11. Fenton Washburn
12. Barbara Mulgravy

Column B
a. lawyer who defended Peter Richards
b. John Ross's psychologist
c. Pam looked appealing while Cliff did the dealing
d. Mark's physician
e. local sheriff
f. new member of the oil cartel
g. part of Edgar Randolph's secret past
h. Cliff's inept oil rigger
i. Bobby bought his oil company
j. Barnes/Wentworth comptroller
k. doctor who handled Sue Ellen's miscarriage
l. fetched a birth certificate for Katherine

Southfork Super Stumpers

Quiz 92
1983—84 Season

1. Pam's secretary, Jackie, has a rarely mentioned last name. What is it?
2. What is Harry McSween's police rank?
3. What architect designed and built Southfork? Why did he visit the Ewings in the fall of 1983?
4. What was the exact title of Edgar Randolph's job in the federal government?
5. Who were Paul Gerber and Harry Green?
6. Whose mother lives in Denton?
7. In what city was Dusty Farlow born?
8. Who drives a black-and-silver Lincoln Continental?
9. Who called who "Stinko"?
10. Who said, "This man can't resist a dare. He was the first man to skydive in the nude"?
11. Who was Miss Kelly?
12. What was the exact amount of Cliff Barnes's bid for the offshore oil tract?
13. Who was Lucas Wade?
14. What did Jessica give J. R. upon her arrival at Southfork?
15. Who is Darius?

Man in the Middle

What men did these pairs of lovely ladies fight over?

1. Sue Ellen _____ Kristin
2. Jenna _____ Pam
3. Bonnie _____ Donna
4. Lucy _____ Sue Ellen
5. Afton _____ Marilee
6. Alicia _____ Sue Ellen
7. Julie _____ Ellie
8. Kristin _____ Lucy
9. Sue Ellen _____ Ellie
10. Pam _____ Katherine

Quick Change Artists

Quiz 94
Test Your *Dallas* IQ

These characters went from rags to riches—or in some cases from milquetoast to manipulator—without much ado. How many of them can you identify?

1. This gossipy club lady turned into a hard-driving business-woman.
2. A shopgirl who blossomed into a beautiful oil exec.
3. She got off the political merry-go-round and found her home on the range.
4. This drifter, drunk, and gambler is now one of California's wealthiest wheeler-dealers.
5. She traded her ratty shirts and jeans for a high-fashion look.
6. This crusading political figure and environmentalist is now a greedy oil man.
7. Once she served up beer and burgers; now it's ensembles and accessories.
8. Devoted to one man for forty-five years, she slowly learned to love another.
9. This randy ranch hand is now a model husband.
10. Deserted her drunken husband, ditched the wrong side of the tracks, and married a Texas millionaire.

Pam's Prince Charmings

Quiz 95
Test Your *Dallas* IQ

Although it seems like Pam loves Bobby first, last, and always, he isn't the only man she's ever been involved with. Can you identify these knights—shining or otherwise—who tried to steal her heart?

1. After they broke up he wound up in a North Vietnamese prison camp.
2. He used to bring Pam to the Southfork barbecues before she married Bobby.
3. Katherine wholeheartedly approved of this match.
4. This Dallas publisher wanted to make romantic headlines with her.
5. Talk about surprises! Pam woke up—and found him in bed with her.
6. He had a strong attachment to Kristin.
7. This college chum of Bobby's made an illegal pass.
8. He made her work overtime—in Paris!
9. This ranch hand's son charmed Bobby and Pam.
10. Pam loved him, but as Sue Ellen told her, "Sometimes love just isn't enough."

Two of a Kind

What do these unlikely pairs have in common?

1. Sue Ellen and Digger
2. Donna and Valene
3. Mavis and Marilee
4. Alan and Kit
5. Agnes and Vicky
6. Rebecca and Mark
7. Pam and Ray
8. Pam and Lucy
9. Holly and Jordan
10. Mrs. Farlow and Mrs. Bradley

Ye Olde Prop Shoppe

Quiz 97
Test Your *Dallas* IQ

What characters would you associate with the following accessories?

1. swim trunks
2. diary
3. cardigan sweaters
4. Porsche
5. camera equipment
6. gold medallion
7. oil map of Texas
8. *Gray's Anatomy*
9. campaign buttons and posters
10. ladies' workout equipment

J. R. Slept Here . . . and There . . . and Everywhere

Quiz 98
Test Your *Dallas* IQ

Column A lists some of J. R.'s occasional bed partners. You'll uncover an interesting fact about each in Column B.

Column A
1. Holly Harwood
2. Serena
3. Katherine Wentworth
4. Afton Cooper
5. Garnet McGee
6. Judy
7. Julie Grey
8. Sue Ellen
9. Kristin
10. Leslie Stewart

Column B
a. J. R. taped their love-making
b. Sue Ellen saw them leaving a Fort Worth hotel
c. she made a big splash in his pool.
d. J. R. only wants her when he can't have her
e. J. R. forgot her birthday and lost her forever
f. she aimed to keep their relations strictly public
g. Sue Ellen caught them in bed together
h. J. R. took her to the Stardrift Lounge
i. she always listens to his problems
j. he cornered her talent— and her "exclusive services"

Supporting Actors

Quiz 99
Test Your *Dallas* IQ

Match the actors in Column A with the roles they played in Column B.

Column A
1. James Whitmore, Jr.
2. Jeff Cooper
3. Terry Lester
4. Mark Wheeler
5. Tom Fuccello
6. Peter Mark Richman
7. Gene Evans
8. Stephen Elliott
9. William Smithers
10. John Zaremba

Column B
a. Scotty Demerest
b. Dave Culver
c. Garrison Southworth
d. Buzz Connors
e. Jeremy Wendell
f. Harlan Danvers
g. Dr. Ellby
h. Kit Mainwaring
i. Maynard Anderson
j. Rudy Millington

Supporting Actresses

Match the actresses in Column A with the roles they played in Column B.

Column A
1. Talia Balsam
2. Alice Hirson
3. Stephanie Blackmore.
4. Lesley Woods
5. Melody Anderson
6. Tricia O'Neil
7. Jeanna Michaels
8. Sheila Larken
9. Laura Johnson
10. Debbie Rennard

Column B
a. Mavis Anderson
b. Sly
c. Barbara Mulgravy
d. Priscilla Duncan
e. Connie
f. Serena
g. Linda Farlow
h. Betty Lou Barker
i. Rita Briggs
j. Amanda Ewing

Guess the Guests

Quiz 101
Test Your *Dallas* IQ

Here are ten more very familiar faces who left their calling cards at Southfork. Match the actors in Column A with their *Dallas* characters in Column B.

Column A
1. Don Porter
2. Charles Siebert
3. Peter Brown
4. Barry Jenner
5. Brian Dennehy
6. Barry Corbin
7. Ted Gehring
8. Fred Beir
9. Jim McKrell
10. Tyler Banks

Column B
a. Lyle Sloan
b. Ben Maxwell
c. Luther Frick
d. John Ross Ewing III
e. Matthew S. Devlin
f. Tom Flintoff
g. Dr. Jerry Kenderson
h. Henry Webster
i. Fenton Washburn
j. Brady York

Two of a Kind (Part II)

Quiz 102
Test Your *Dallas* IQ

What do these unlikely pairs have in common?

1. Valene and Jenna
2. Maynard and Punk
3. Sue Ellen and Clayton
4. Scotty Demerest and Cliff Barnes
5. Jordan Lee and J. R. (not a business connection)
6. Dusty and J. R. (not their involvement with Sue Ellen)
7. Julie and Hutch
8. Bobby and John Ross
9. Sue Ellen and Pam (a medical problem)
10. Christopher's father and Pam's first husband

Everything You Wanted to Know About Sue Ellen . . . But Were Afraid to Ask

Quiz 103
Test Your *Dallas* IQ

Decide if the following statements are true or false.

1. Sue Ellen was first runner-up in the Miss America contest.
2. The only thing Sue Ellen remembered about her father was "the smell of liquor on his breath."
3. Sue Ellen never helps Miss Ellie in the kitchen.
4. When Sue Ellen was voted Miss Texas, J. R. was one of the pageant judges.
5. Sue Ellen partially blamed her mother for Kristin's death.
6. Sue Ellen's frigidity destroyed her first marriage to J. R.
7. On two different occasions Sue Ellen has survived near fatal car crashes.
8. Her father died when Kristin was a year old.
9. Sue Ellen is obsessed with giving John Ross a little brother or sister.
10. For the first seven years that she lived at Southfork, Sue Ellen and Bobby barely said more than hello to each other every day.

Trivial Togetherness (Part I)

Quiz 104
Test Your *Dallas* IQ

Which of these pairs of characters actually shared a scene together? Simply answer true or false.

1. Digger and Miss Ellie
2. Digger and Rebecca
3. Donna and Sam Culver
4. Dusty Farlow and Garnet McGee
5. Jock and Mickey Trotter
6. Bobby and Liz Craig
7. Aunt Lil and Aunt Maggie
8. J. R. and Patricia Shepard
9. Jenna and Sue Ellen
10. Lucy and Alex Ward

Trivial Togetherness (Part II)

Quiz 105
Test Your *Dallas* IQ

Which of these pairs of characters actually shared a scene together? Simply answer true or false.

1. Gary Ewing and Garrison Southworth
2. J. R. and Edgar Randolph
3. Julie Grey and Miss Ellie
4. Jenna and Renaldo Marchetta
5. Clint Ogden and Katherine Wentworth
6. Jock and Holly Harwood
7. Rebecca Wentworth and Jessica Montford
8. Kristin and Christopher
9. Lucy and Evelyn Michaelson
10. Bobby and Charlie

Dangerous Documents

Quiz 106
Test Your *Dallas* IQ

Here are ten missives and messages that played a fateful hand in *Dallas* happenings. In each case name the author.

1. The letter that broke up Pam and Bobby's marriage.
2. This diary helped Donna solve the mystery of Uncle Jonas.
3. It gave permission to drill for oil on Section 40 of Southfork.
4. It pitted J. R. against Bobby in a year-long business battle.
5. This diary explained the secrets of the Southern Cross.
6. It said in part, ". . . it's important for me to go out while I can still call myself a man."
7. It gave Miss Ellie a controlling share of Ewing Oil.
8. "He is unharmed and will not be hurt as long as everyone cooperates. . . . Cliff Barnes is to act as the go-between."
9. "I do know where the skeletons are buried. I've been hurt enough. I'm ready to sell."
10. This piece of paper confirmed the sale of one-third of Wentworth Tool and Die for $18 million.

Nicknames and Slick Names

Quiz 107
Test Your *Dallas* IQ

1. Who is Sylvia?
2. What character's middle name is James?
3. Who is Charlotte?
4. What is Punk's real name?
5. What character's middle name is Southworth?
6. What was the full name of Pam's first husband (all three names)?
7. How was Michael more commonly known at Southfork?
8. What character, besides Dave Culver, was named Dave?
9. What was Jock's full name?
10. What was Christopher's first name on his original birth certificate?

Two of a Kind (Part III)

Quiz 108
Test Your *Dallas* IQ

What do these unlikely pairs have in common?

1. Jock and J. R. (a medical condition)
2. Franklin Horner and Vaughn Leland
3. Dr. Waring and Mr. Crutcher
4. Leann Rees and Jenna Wade
5. Afton Cooper and Garnet McGee
6. Amanda and Margaret
7. Justin Carlisle and Craig Stewart
8. Patricia and Arliss
9. Willie Gust and Roger Larson
10. Beau Middens and Mickey Trotter

Gender Loving Care

Quiz 109
Test Your *Dallas* IQ

In each case tell whether the medic is male or female.

1. Waring
2. Danvers
3. Lacey
4. Ellby
5. Krane
6. Ward
7. Jeffries
8. Hopkins
9. Kenderson
10. Conrad

Jumbled Geography

Quiz 110
Test Your *Dallas* IQ

1. After losing her court battle to overturn Jock's will, Miss Ellie went to recuperate in _____.
2. Henry Montford lived in _____.
3. In order to get in touch with Thornton McLeish, Bobby had to place a long-distance call to _____.
4. _____ held special romantic memories for Mark and Pam.
5. Garcia was J. R.'s contact in _____.
6. Perez was J. R.'s contact in _____.
7. _____ was the first stop on Jock and Ellie's second honeymoon.
8. Christopher was born in _____.
9. Rebecca was on her way to _____ when her plane crashed.
10. Ray and Donna were on their way to _____ when Aunt Lil phoned.

Three's Company

When it comes to getting physical, J. R., Ray, and Cliff have three of the raunchiest reputations in Dallas. Tell which of the trio each of these ladies has enjoyed a physical relationship with.

1. Sue Ellen
2. Afton Cooper
3. Katherine Wentworth
4. Marilee Stone
5. Holly Harwood
6. Donna
7. Garnet McGee
8. Julie Grey
9. Jenna Wade
10. Kristin

J. R. vs. Bobby

Quiz 112
Test Your *Dallas* IQ

Was it J. R. or Bobby who was responsible for each of these events?

1. He entered a foreign country illegally.
2. He set George Hicks up with a call girl.
3. He saved his brother's life when their plane crashed.
4. He told Holly Harwood, "I'd like to toast the fact that you'll never be my sister-in-law."
5. He courted his ex-wife with jewelry, flowers, and a video cassette.
6. He served in the state senate.
7. He almost ran for the U.S. Senate.
8. During the year-long battle for control of Ewing Oil, his half of the company earned over $50 million.
9. He put two pistols in Walt Driscoll's attaché case.
10. He wasn't home when the fire at Southfork started.

John Ross vs. Christopher

Quiz 113
Test Your *Dallas* IQ

Identify which Ewing grandson each of these statements describes.

1. He is the older of the two.
2. He was born via cesarean section.
3. He has an aunt who loves to bring him water toys.
4. He does not live with either of his natural parents.
5. He was born prematurely.
6. He has lived in two different states.
7. He frequently visits his daddy's office.
8. He recently became very interested in swimming.
9. He never saw his Granddaddy Jock.
10. False statements about his paternity actually appeared in a Dallas newspaper.

Miss Ellie vs. Rebecca

Quiz 114
Test Your *Dallas* IQ

Tell which of these statements apply to Ellie Ewing, to Rebecca Wentworth, to both women, or to neither of them.

1. Gave birth to five children.
2. Married twice.
3. Romantically involved with Digger Barnes.
4. Romantically involved with Clayton Farlow.
5. Romantically involved with Harrison Page.
6. Christopher's grandmother.
7. Former resident of Houston.
8. Forgave Pam for divorcing Bobby.
9. Romantically involved with Brooks Oliver.
10. Close friends with Mavis Anderson.

Sue Ellen vs. Pam

Quiz 115
Test Your *Dallas* IQ

Decide if Sue Ellen or Pam is the subject of each of these statements.

1. She has no career
2. She has never been an unfaithful wife.
3. She has a half-sister.
4. It took Miss Ellie a while to accept her as a daughter-in-law.
5. Following her divorce she had a hard time learning to live on her own.
6. She hired a detective to find her mother.
7. Cliff tried to palm her off on a man named Ben Kesey.
8. She moves in and out of her husband's bedroom.
9. Her marriage broke Julie's heart.
10. She almost married someone out of compassion, not love.

Ray vs. Gary

Quiz 116
Test Your *Dallas* IQ

Decide if Ray or Gary is the subject of each of these statements.

1. He was the product of a wartime romance.
2. He took a job as a blackjack dealer to overcome a gambling problem.
3. He reconciled with his wife after a seventeen-year separation.
4. He has no children.
5. He has only been married once.
6. He helped Bobby put "the sting" on Walt Driscoll.
7. Miss Ellie paid for his home.
8. He was "the skinniest kid of fifteen" that Jock had ever seen.
9. He refuses to live like a millionaire.
10. According to Jock's will he can only spend the interest from his inheritance for the first four years after Jock's demise.

Julie, Sly, or Kristin

Quiz 117
Test Your *Dallas* IQ

Identify the famous—or should we say infamous?—Ewing Oil secretary who best fits each of these descriptions.

1. The color red got her in a lot of trouble.
2. She wanted to get her brother out of prison.
3. Her mother pushed her into J. R.'s arms.
4. Thanks to her double-agentry, Cliff got his offshore oil tract.
5. She's the only one of the three who ever worked with Phyllis.
6. J. R. hired her before she ever set foot inside the office.
7. The boss's father liked to take her out to lunch.
8. Even when he caught her spying, J. R. didn't fire her.
9. Her relationship with J. R. was strictly business.
10. She's the only one who's still alive.

Three of a Kind

Quiz 118
Test Your *Dallas* IQ

What do these tricky trios have in common?

1. Pam, Cliff, and Katherine
2. Lucy, John Ross, and Christopher
3. Pam, Cliff, and Edgar Randolph
4. Travis Boyd, Holly Harwood, and Wade Luce
5. Ray, Bobby, and Gary
6. Charles Eccles, Lyle Sloan, and Kyle Bennett
7. Cliff, Jenna, and Kristin
8. Rebecca, Ellie, and Marilee
9. Amanda, Pam, and Jonas
10. Liz, Jackie, and Pam

Mitch vs. Mickey

Quiz 119
Test Your *Dallas* IQ

Decide if Mitch Cooper or Mickey Trotter is the man described in each of these statements.

1. A native Southerner.
2. Lucy rescued him from a barroom brawl.
3. He helped start a brawl between J. R. and Cliff.
4. The man in Lucy's life before Roger Larson.
5. His mother disapproved of his romance with Lucy.
6. A wealthy, older woman found him very attractive.
7. The studious type.
8. Worked as a gas station attendant.
9. Tennis was his game.
10. Had an arrest record.

Jock vs. Clayton

Quiz 120
Test Your *Dallas* IQ

Tell which of these statements apply to Jock Ewing, or to Clayton Farlow, or to both men, or have nothing to do with either of them.

1. Survived coronary insufficiency.
2. Had to rebuild his ranch from scratch after a devastating fire.
3. His son is a drifter.
4. Married a Southworth.
5. Once in love with Amy.
6. Once in love with Sue Ellen.
7. Once in love with Sue Ellen's mother.
8. Went to Europe with Miss Ellie.
9. His daughter lives in New York.
10. Both an oil man and a rancher.

A Burst of Firsts

Quiz 121
Test Your *Dallas* IQ

Here are the first names of twenty characters who have appeared in *Dallas* since 1978. How many of their last names can you still recall?

1. Travis
2. Vaughn
3. Thornton
4. Harv
5. Brady
6. Alan
7. Harlan
8. Amos
9. Blair
10. Hutch
11. Sam
12. Jordan
13. Gil
14. Walt
15. Willy Joe
16. Garrison
17. Arthur
18. Jeff
19. Edgar
20. Kyle

Lucy vs. Afton

Quiz 122
Test Your *Dallas* IQ

Tell which of these statements apply to Lucy, or to Afton, to both, or to neither of them.

1. Has never been married.
2. Is devoted to Pam.
3. Occasionally visits her folks in California.
4. Attended college.
5. Had an affair with Mark Graison.
6. Had an affair with Charles Eccles.
7. Is less than enthusiastic about Chinese food.
8. Has singing talent.
9. Is a multimillionairess in her own right.
10. Was in love with Mickey Trotter.

In Order of Appearance (Part I)

Quiz 123
Test Your *Dallas* IQ

In each case decide which actress arrived on *Dallas* first.

1. Charlene Tilton/Susan Howard
2. Morgan Fairchild/Priscilla Presley
3. Fern Fitzgerald/Morgan Brittany
4. Alexis Smith/Priscilla Pointer
5. Lois Chiles/Joan Van Ark
6. Donna Reed/Barbara Bel Geddes
7. Audrey Landers/Kate Reid
8. Victoria Principal/Linda Gray
9. Tina Louise/Susan Flannery
10. Shalane McCall/Mary Crosby

In Order of Appearance (Part II)

Quiz 124
Test Your *Dallas IQ*

In each case decide which actor arrived in Dallas first.

1. Howard Keel/Jared Martin
2. Patrick Duffy/Larry Hagman
3. Leigh McCloskey/Timothy Patrick Murphy
4. Christopher Atkins/John Beck
5. Keenan Wynn/William Windom
6. George O. Petrie/Martin E. Brooks
7. Steve Kanaly/Randolph Powell
8. Dennis Patrick/Ken Kercheval
9. Morgan Woodward/Ben Piazza
10. Jim Davis/David Wayne

Those Unforgettable Scenes in . . .
Bobby's Office

Quiz 125
Test Your *Dallas* IQ

Which of these scenes took place in Bobby's office at Ewing Oil?

1. Bobby was shot.
2. J. R. was shot.
3. Katherine gave Bobby a *very* sisterly kiss on the cheek.
4. Thornton McLeish brought Bobby a risky deal.
5. Pam and Bobby agreed to end their marriage.
6. Bobby was kidnapped.
7. Donna showed J. R. her power of attorney to act as co-president of Ewing Oil.
8. Bobby called Pam at the Store to cancel one more luncheon date.
9. A likely place to find Phyllis.
10. Bobby was here when J. R. was shot.

Those Unforgettable Scenes at the Southfork Barbecues

Quiz 126
Test Your *Dallas* IQ

Which of these scenes took place at one of Miss Ellie's annual Southfork barbecues?

1. Word came that Jock's plane had crashed.
2. Sue Ellen renewed her acquaintance with Clint Ogden.
3. Digger came to make peace with Jock.
4. Miss Ellie's brother returned from the dead.
5. Pam had a miscarriage.
6. J. R. was almost lynched by his fellow oil men.
7. Gary returned home after a seventeen-year absence.
8. Miss Ellie vowed to end the war between J. R. and Bobby.
9. Miss Ellie removed J. R. as head of Ewing Oil.
10. Christopher was kidnapped.

Those Unforgettable Scenes . . .
J. R. and Sue Ellen's Bedroom

Quiz 127
Test Your *Dallas* IQ

Which of these scenes took place in J. R. and Sue Ellen's bedroom suite?

1. J. R. cavorted with Holly Harwood.
2. J. R. cavorted with Afton.
3. Sue Ellen was trapped there when Southfork went up in flames.
4. Peter Richards spent the night there.
5. J. R. stayed there while Sue Ellen moved into another room.
6. Dusty hid in a closet.
7. The gun that shot J. R. was hidden there.
8. John Ross was conceived there.
9. Kristin moved in when Sue Ellen moved out.
10. J. R. accused Sue Ellen of using him like some stud service.

Chock Full of Challengers

Quiz 128
Test Your *Dallas* IQ

1. How many barrels of oil did J. R. ship to Cuba?
2. Who went by the code name "Miss Wells" when she phoned Cliff?
3. After Renaldo Marchetta left Rome, in what South American country did he reside for a while?
4. Mark once offered to take Pam on a weekend trip to Tahiti. How would they get there?
5. Who smiled and suggested that Ellie might fall down a flight of stairs? Before what big event?
6. What couple invited all the Ewings to their fortieth anniversary party?
7. Jenna Wade has held three different jobs. Name them.
8. Who told Pam that she was going to Los Angeles to see a sick friend of her father's? Who was she really planning to visit there?
9. Aside from a few scratches and some loss of blood, what other injury did Sue Ellen suffer when she had her miscarriage?
10. How old was Barbara Mulgravy when she was molested by Edgar Randolph?

Familiar Faces in Different Places

Quiz 129
Test Your *Dallas* IQ

Match the *Dallas* stars in Column A with the TV series (Column B) on which they regularly appeared.

Column A
1. Linda Gray
2. Susan Howard
3. Patrick Duffy
4. Larry Hagman
5. John Beck
6. Morgan Brittany
7. Priscilla Beaulieu Presley
8. Leigh McCloskey

Column B
a. *The Man from Atlantis*
b. *Glitter*
c. *All That Glitters*
d. *Executive Suite*
e. *Petrocelli*
f. *Those Amazing Animals*
g. *I Dream of Jeannie*
h. *Flamingo Road*

Setside Confidential

Quiz 130
Test Your *Dallas* IQ

1. On what three nights of the week has *Dallas* aired on CBS?
2. Which two *Dallas* guest stars have since teamed up on another CBS show that also features Kevin Dobson and Michele Lee?
3. Before Martin E. Brooks became Edgar Randolph, he was a regular on both *Six Million Dollar Man* and *Bionic Woman*. What role did he portray on those shows?
4. For many years TV viewers knew her as "Donna Stone." Who is she?
5. This actor was featured in Pam's story line, then became a star of *Falcon Crest*. Can you place him?
6. This early *Dallas* guest star now headlines on *Hill Street Blues*. Who is she?
7. How many brand-new episodes of *Dallas* aired in the 1983–84 TV season?
8. Barbara Bel Geddes and Barry Nelson teamed in the long-running Broadway hit, *Mary, Mary*. How were they reunited on *Dallas*?
9. Which two *Dallas* principals both appeared in the movie, *The Life and Times of Judge Roy Bean*?
10. Which *Dallas* star was actually born in the city where Sue Ellen and Dusty used to meet secretly?

More Missing Persons

Quiz 131
Test Your *Dallas* IQ

1. Lucy went to Jan Higgins to arrange a modeling job for _____.
2. Clayton stiffened when Ellie suggested inviting _____ to their wedding.
3. _____ only bid $103 million on the government offshore oil tract that went to Cliff.
4. When Jenna and Bobby broke up, _____ came to Bobby's office to tell him how badly she felt.
5. _____ kept Pam and Bobby from going to the Andersons' anniversary party together.
6. _____ quickly returned from Europe when Bobby was shot.
7. _____has been arrested for the murder of _____, the shooting of _____, and the shooting of _____.
8. _____ loaned Cliff over $200 million at 18% interest.
9. _____ gave Pam a beautiful strand of pearls.
10. At the same time that _____ toasted the Ewings and the Farlows, _____ toasted Pam and Mark's impending marriage.

Trials and Trivializations (Part I)

Quiz 132
Test Your *Dallas* IQ

1. What was the name of Cliff's offshore oil tract?
2. How much higher was Cliff's bid for that tract than J. R.'s bid?
3. What medical problem did Bobby develop as a result of being shot?
4. Who stopped Katherine from visiting Bobby in the hospital?
5. Who begged Pam not to keep visiting Bobby while he was ill?
6. On the night of the shooting why had Bobby gone into J. R.'s office?
7. Who found Bobby after the shooting had taken place?
8. Who had to be given oxygen after they were trapped in the Southfork fire?
9. How did Clayton find out about the Southfork fire?
10. Who is Miss Gillis?

Trials and Trivializations (Part II)

Quiz 133
Test Your *Dallas* IQ

1. Did Miss Ellie testify at the hearing to overturn Jock's will?
2. Who sent for the fire engines when Southfork went up in flames?
3. What news did J. R. and Katherine toast together?
4. How did Miss Ellie find out about the fire at Southfork?
5. Did Mickey ever regain consciousness before he died?
6. How severe was Mickey's paralysis?
7. Pam once brought Cliff a photograph. Of whom? Why?
8. When he was hospitalized, what unusual item did Bobby start wearing?
9. When Katherine forged the ''Dear John'' letter that broke up Pam and Bobby's marriage, how did she get Pam to sign it?
10. To whom was that phony letter supposedly written? What did it say?

Trials and Trivializations (Part III)

Quiz 134
Test Your *Dallas* IQ

1. What was John Ross's main problem at summer camp?
2. Shortly before he died, who did Mickey tell not to visit him anymore?
3. How did Donna first become acquainted with Paul Morgan?
4. What foursome spent a fun evening at an all-night hamburger stand?
5. To what woman does J. R. occasionally reveal his deepest secrets?
6. Did Pam and Bobby both appear at their divorce hearing?
7. What did Sue Ellen tell Lucy that all the Ewing women have in common?
8. Which of Pam's relatives was described by everyone as "a very religious" person?
9. Who beat J. R. out on the Murphy oil deal?
10. Of all the women in Bobby's life, who is the only one who ever got J. R.'s seal of approval?

Southfork Super Bowl—For *Dallas* Experts Only (Part I)

Quiz 135
Test Your *Dallas* IQ

1. When did Pam and Mark make love for the first time?
2. In what city did Katherine offer to set Jenna up in business?
3. Who bought Ben Kesey's company?
4. What did Mark do just before he carried Pam off to his bedroom for the first time?
5. What three women competed in the mechanical bull-riding contest at Billy Bob's?
6. While Miss Ellie was out of town with Clayton, who planned the annual Southfork barbecue?
7. Who worried that she might only be "window dressing" in her new job?
8. What *Dallas* character has lived in Italy, Malibu, South America, and Montreal?
9. Which of Jock's sons testified at the hearing to overturn his will?
10. Who loves electric trains?

Southfork Super Bowl—For *Dallas* Experts Only (Part II)

Quiz 136
Test Your *Dallas* IQ

1. Miss Ellie once sat in her kitchen making out a list for Clayton. What did the list contain?
2. How much was Cliff's share of Wentworth Tool and Die actually worth when he sold it to Katherine?
3. Who rescued Edgar Randolph just in time when he tried to commit suicide?
4. During her divorce from J. R., what kind of house did Sue Ellen live in?
5. Who introduced Bobby to Holly Harwood?
6. What government organization did the Texas Energy Commission replace?
7. When Lucy learned of her pregnancy, in whom did she confide?
8. Why did Ray and Donna originally plan a trip to New York?
9. Who performed Lucy's abortion?
10. Aside from her swimming pool and her bedroom, where else did Holly Harwood like to do business?

Southfork Super Bowl—For *Dallas* Experts Only (Part III)

Quiz 137
Test Your *Dallas* IQ

1. After his marriage Dusty returned home once. Where did he and Sue Ellen have a few moments alone together?
2. What was the one thing that Mickey lacked in Kansas?
3. What event had prompted Dusty's marriage to Linda?
4. Who introduced Ellie to Frank Crutcher?
5. Why was Mickey arrested in Kansas?
6. According to the codicil to Jock's will, what would have happened if J. R. or Bobby had died during the year of the contest?
7. What was J. R.'s toast to Bobby after hearing that stipulation?
8. Aside from the division of ownership, there was one other stipulation about Ewing Oil in Jock's will. What was it?
9. There were two women Rebecca didn't want her son involved with. Who were they?
10. What was Mickey's first job at Southfork?

Southfork Super Bowl—For *Dallas* Experts Only (Part IV)

Quiz 138
Test Your *Dallas* IQ

1. Carol Driscoll was on her way home from what appointment when the fake hit-and-run accident occurred?
2. Who set up Carol's phony accident for J. R.?
3. Who was Bobby's competitor for the McLeish brothers' oil deal?
4. After J. R. got his oil variance where did he send Walt Driscoll?
5. Afton eventually became an entertainer at what posh Dallas club?
6. The first time he asked Lucy out, where did Mickey want to take Lucy?
7. What did Miss Ellie serve the first time Clayton visited Southfork?
8. What was the McLeish brothers' biggest problem in drilling for oil?
9. What made J. R. Ewing an instant media hero and a potential national political figure?
10. Where did Pam and Mark meet for the first time alone? What did they share?

Southfork Super Bowl—For *Dallas* Experts Only (Part V)

Quiz 139
Test Your *Dallas* IQ

1. The first time Afton dined with Cliff in his new condo, they watched a memorable TV program. What was it?
2. Who was the first person to encourage Mark Graison to pursue Pam?
3. How much did the cartel pay Bobby for the Wellington field?
4. What did Sue Ellen ask Clayton on J. R.'s behalf?
5. What did Bobby use Wendy for?
6. What was George Hicks's secret habit?
7. Why did Cliff get roaring drunk and miss his plane flight on the day his mother died?
8. Who was Mike Hughes?
9. Who moved into a suite at the Fairview Hotel?
10. Where did the reading of Rebecca's will take place?

Take a Movie Break

Quiz 140
Test Your *Dallas* IQ

Name the *Dallas* star who appeared in each of these feature films or made-for-television movies.

1. *Seven Brides for Seven Brothers.*
2. *Enola Gay*
3. *The Blue Lagoon*
4. *Dairy of a Teenage Hitchhiker*
5. *Vertigo*
6. *The Way We Were*
7. *Audrey Rose*
8. *Not in Front of the Children*
9. *To Find My Son*
10. *Not Just Another Affair*

Southfork Super Bowl—For *Dallas* Experts Only (Part VI)

Quiz 141
Test Your *Dallas* IQ

1. What does Miss Ellie write for Teresa?
2. What was found along with Walt Driscoll's corpse?
3. Who would you expect to find at Turtle Creek?
4. What was the nationality on Walt Driscoll's phony passport?
5. Who first told Sue Ellen that J. R. and Holly Harwood were having an affair?
6. What incriminating item of clothing made Sue Ellen believe her?
7. What was Holly's financial loss, thanks to J. R.?
8. In Cuba J. R. was finally paid for his oil in the form of a Swiss bank draft. What was the amount?
9. Where did Sue Ellen spend the night after finding J. R. in Holly's bed?
10. According to J. R., what were Bobby's "frozen assets"?

Family Ties

Quiz 142
Test Your *Dallas* IQ

What on-screen relationships do these pairs of performers share?

1. Patrick Duffy/Steve Kanaly
2. Priscilla Beaulieu Presley/Shalane McCall
3. Victoria Principal/Morgan Brittany
4. Donna Reed/Howard Keel
5. Susan Howard/Tom Fuccello
6. Donna Reed/Charlene Tilton
7. Ken Kercheval/Victoria Principal
8. Audrey Landers/Leigh McCloskey
9. Larry Hagman/Charlene Tilton
10. Linda Gray/Ted Shackelford

Ail, Ail, The Gang's All Here!

Quiz 143
Test Your Soap Opera IQ

Match the actors in Column A with the on-screen medical complications they endured in Column B.

Column A
1. Patrick Duffy
2. Charlene Tilton
3. Victoria Principal
4. Keenan Wynn
5. Barbara Bel Geddes
6. Tyler Banks
7. Larry Hagman
8. Ken Kercheval
9. Patricia McCormack
10. Lesley Woods

Column B
a. premature birth
b. mastectomy
c. neurofibromatosis
d. blindness
e. ruptured spleen
f. incurable insanity
g. overdose of pills and liquor
h. abortion
i. miscarriage
j. cosmetic surgery

Southfork Super Bowl—For *Dallas* Experts Only (Part VII)

Quiz 144
Test Your *Dallas* IQ

1. What made Jenna feel like a "kept woman"?
2. What brother and sister did J. R. ask Harry McSween to investigate?
3. What did Cliff pay Sly $10,000 for?
4. What did J. R. hire Peter Richards to do?
5. What fatal disease did Mark Graison contract?
6. Who did Bobby take out on a date for an ice cream?
7. Who was the first Ewing to suspect that Jessica was demented?
8. Who tried to attack J. R. after Bobby was shot?
9. Who got the call when Cliff's offshore oil tract came in?
10. Who is the only Ewing son who has never been an assassin's target?

Answers

Quiz 1
1. Sue Ellen said it about J. R. after she caught him in bed with Holly Harwood. 2. Chinese food. 3. $1,000. 4. traveling in the Orient. 5. six years; 6. Morgan Fairchild, Francine Tacker, and Priscilla Beaulieu Presley. 7. Jock; she suffered from insanity and had to be institutionalized. 8. Afton. 9. Thornton McLeish; $26 million. 10. J. R. was shot by an unknown assailant.

Quiz 2
1. Patrick Duffy. 2. Victoria Principal. 3. Larry Hagman. 4. Jim Davis. 5. Barbara Bel Geddes. 6. Linda Gray. 7. Charlene Tilton. 8 Steve Kanaly. 9. Ken Kercheval. 10. Susan Howard. 11. Howard Keel. 12. Donna Reed.

Quiz 3

1. Jock and Ellie Ewing. 2. Hutch McKinney and Rebecca Wentworth. 3. Renaldo Marchetta and Jenna Wade. 4. Jock and Ellie Ewing. 5. J. R. and Sue Ellen Ewing. 6. Jeff Farraday and Kristin Shepard. 7. Digger Barnes and Rebecca Wentworth. 8. Herbert and Rebecca Wentworth. 9. Gary and Valene Ewing. 10. Jock Ewing and Margaret Krebbs.

Quiz 4

1. d. 2. g. 3. a. 4. c. 5. i. 6. f. 7. j. 8. e. 9. h. 10. b.

Quiz 5

1. Linda. 2. Carol. 3. Martha. 4. Mavis. 5. Alicia. 6. Henry. 7. Marilee. 8. Margaret. 9. Leslie. 10. DeeDee.

Quiz 6

1. e. 2. d. 3. g. 4. a. 5. h. 6. i. 7. j. 8. b. 9. f. 10. c.

Quiz 7

1. Braddock Road. 2. Miss Ellie's barbecue. 3. Pam. 4. he played poker with the cops. 5. Bobby, Jenna, Charlie, and Christopher. 6. yellow. 7. Katherine Wentworth. 8. Barbara Bel Geddes. 9. Daughters of the Alamo. 10. Westar and Four State.

Quiz 8

1. Sue Ellen's housekeeper (during her divorce from J. R.). 2. they slept with J. R., which damaged their reputations in Bobby's eyes. 3. J. R. 4. Pam. 5. she sued them for fraud and wrongful death of her husband; she sought a $10 million

judgment. 6. Jenna Wade. 7. the death of Pam's mother. 8. Sam Culver and Jock Ewing. 9. on a highway heading for California; a police helicopter tracked them down. 10. the woman who raised Pam and Cliff.

Quiz 9

1. Emporia, Kansas. 2. Peter's mother. 3. in a hotel suite. 4. Lucy's photographer. 5. Smithfield and Bennett. 6. Jock. 7. Dusty. 8. Barnes/Wentworth/Graisco. 9. Takapa Lake. 10. Miss Ellie.

Quiz 10

1. f. 2. g. 3. e. 4. i. 5. c. 6. h. 7. a. 8. j. 9. b. 10. d.

Quiz 11

1. Jessica Montford. 2. Lilimae Clements. 3. Donna Krebbs. 4. Ray Krebbs. 5. Katherine Wentworth (or Sue Ellen Ewing, since Kristin was his natural mother). 6. J. R. Ewing. 7. Abby Ewing. 8. Jamie Ewing. 9. Mitch Cooper. 10. Bobby Ewing.

Quiz 12

1. Harv Smithfield. 2. Garrett McLeish. 3. Garrison Southworth. 4. Arliss Cooper. 5. Dusty Farlow. 6. Christopher Ewing. 7. Lucy Ewing. 8. Mickey Trotter. 9. Sly Lovegren. 10. Bobby Ewing.

Quiz 13

1. Katherine. 2. Cliff. 3. Rebecca Wentworth. 4. Gil Thurman.

5. Pam. 6. J. R. 7. Mitch. 8. Mark Graison. 9. Marilee Stone. 10. Bobby.

Quiz 14
1. Marshall, Texas. 2. they were killed in a car accident. 3. Sam Culver; Governor of Texas and Speaker of the House. 4. their mutual concern for the environment, as members of the DOA, brought them together. 5. at City Hall in Dallas. 6. Pam and Bobby. 7. at Ray's house on Southfork. 8. the Takapa Development Project; Ray favored it; Donna opposed it. 9. biographies. 10. Sam Culver.

Quiz 15
1. J. R. 2. J. R. 3. Dusty Farlow. 4. Clint Ogden. 5. Dr. Ellby. 6. Roy Ralston. 7. Cliff Barnes. 8. Peter Richards. 9. Clayton Farlow. 10. Arthur Elrod.

Quiz 16
1. a. 2. c. 3. c. 4. c. 5. b. 6. b. 7. a. 8. c. 9. a. 10. c.

Quiz 17
1. d. 2. g. 3. e. 4. i. 5. f. 6, a. 7. c. 8. b. 9. j. 10. h.

Quiz 18
1. Jock, J. R. 2. Lucy. 3. Julie, Sue Ellen. 4. Bobby. 5. Ray. 6. Pam. 7. Cliff. 8. Lucy, Miss Ellie. 9. J. R., Ray. 10. Pam's. 11. Miss Ellie, Sue Ellen. 12. Lucy. 13. Bobby, Cliff. 14. Jock, Bobby. 15. J. R.

Quiz 19

1. migraines. 2. sexy negligee. 3. busboy. 4. hayloft. 5. file. 6. dress. 7. letter. 8. helicopter. 9. nursery. 10. Austin. 11. rododex card. 12. carpenters (building shelves).

Quiz 20

1. the caterers. 2. Digger; Jock. 3. Pam's pregnancy. 4. he was on the wagon. 5. his fortune and his sweetheart (Miss Ellie). 6. 15. 7. Jock; marriage to Miss Ellie and ownership of Southfork. 8. she slipped off a ladder in the hayloft. 9. J. R. (he had been arguing with Pam in the loft). 10. Jock.

Quiz 21

1. David Ackroyd. 2. Joan Van Ark. 3. David Wayne. 4. Kate Mulgrew. 5. Colleen Camp. 6. Tina Louise. 7. Martha Scott. 8. Veronica Hamel. 9. Barbara Babcock. 10. Greg Evigan.

Quiz 22.

1. J. R., Gary, and Bobby. 2. J. R. (oldest); Bobby (youngest). 3. J. R. 4. Ellie's brother, Garrison. 5. Bobby. 6. Gary. 7. Mercedes; EWING 3. 8. Gary. 9. Bobby. 10. Bobby. 11. Gary. 12. J. R. 13. Gary. 14. Bobby. 15. J. R.

Quiz 23

1. Jock and Ellie; Jock usually lost. 2. red; EWING 4. 3. needlepoint and crossword puzzles. 4. Lucy. 5. Jock. 6. a bottle of gin. 7. Corvette. 8. her three sons. 9. Sue Ellen. 10. Lucy. 11. it was Cliff's favorite color. 12. Lucy. 13. football (as a quarterback). 14. the Ewings' family physician. 15. to get Jock to marry her.

Quiz 24.
1. Ann. 2. government. 3. he was a homosexual. 4. her mother (Val). 5. a brand-new sportscar. 6. Ray Krebbs. 7. birthday party. 8. J. R. 9. Pam. 10. the senior prom. 11. Jimmy Monahan. 12. "hooker."

Quiz 25
1. f. 2. h. 3. i. 4. g. 5. c. 6. d. 7. j. 8. b. 9. a. 10. e.

Quiz 26
1. g. 2. f. 3. e. 4. h. 5. j. 6. i. 7. c. 8. b. 9. a. 10. d.

Quiz 27
1. to die (and to spend his last days with Miss Ellie). 2. it contained a record of J. R.'s illegal payoffs, pictures of judges and politicians in compromising positions, plus a phony codicil to Jock's will (giving J. R. drilling rights to Section 40 of Southfork); Julie Grey stole the red file. 3. Pam had eloped with Ed Haynes. 4. Donna Culver; Pam and Bobby were shocked because Donna was a married woman. 5. she was photographed in the same bed with Ben Maxwell and Leann Rees; it was false (J. R. had set her up). 6. his girl friend, Jennifer Ames, had died after an illegal abortion. 7. J. R. 8. she found Sue Ellen's scarf in Cliff's apartment. 9. in a Washington hotel room with a party girl. 10. he feared that in her drunken state she might reveal that Cliff Barnes had probably fathered her baby.

Quiz 28
1. $100 million. 2. Cliff. 3. a painting of the old family ranch house. 4. Fletcher Sanitarium. 5. Jock. 6. Kit Mainwaring's parents. 7. breakfast. 8. a sandwich (he knew Cliff wasn't a

big spender). 9. her boss, Liz Craig, wanted her to go on a buying trip for the Store. 10. Gary and Valene. 11. Cliff. 12. buying Rita Briggs's baby. 13. Sue Ellen's mother. 14. Leann (during her call-girl days). 15. J. R. (about Sue Ellen).

Quiz 29
1. a. 2. c. 3. b. 4. c. 5. a. 6. c. 7. c. 8. a. 9. b. 10. b.

Quiz 30
1. he had the opportunity (his fingerprints were found in her apartment) and a possible motive (the red file might have contained incriminating information about Cliff). 2. the message Julie had left on Cliff's answering machine. 3. Julie's message was: "I know where the skeletons are buried . . . I'm ready to sell"; the police thought she was blackmailing Cliff; she actually wanted to help him ruin J. R. 4. in an attaché case she had left at a pawn shop. 5. a pawn ticket and the key to the attaché case. 6. she fell from the roof of her building. 7. Jeb Ames and Willy Joe Garr. 8. assistant D.A. (Sloan); Cliff's defense attorney (Young). 9. during his investigation of Senator Orloff. 10. the phony codicil to Jock's will.

Quiz 31
1. Jock. 2. Bobby. 3. Miss Ellie. 4. J. R. (speaking to Sam Culver). 5. Jock. 6. Julie Grey. 7. Pam (speaking to J. R. and Jock). 8. Cliff (speaking to Sue Ellen). 9. Pam (speaking about her father). 10. Cliff (speaking to Pam).

Quiz 32
1. c. 2. f. 3. h. 4. g. 5. i. 6. d. 7. b. 8. j. 9. e. 10. a.

Quiz 33

1. Randolph Powell. 2. Mary Crosby. 3. Keenan Wynn. 4. Jared Martin. 5. Morgan Woodward. 6. Dennis Patrick. 7. Don Starr. 8. Ted Shackelford. 9. George Petrie. 10. Mel Ferrer.

Quiz 34

1. John Ross Ewing III. 2. in the hospital nursery. 3. the nurse hired by the Ewings to care for John Ross. 4. Cliff. 5. Jeb Ames and Willy Joe Garr; they had just been paroled from jail. 6. $1 million. 7. in a carriage by the waterfall in Thanksgiving Square. 8. Priscilla Duncan. 9. standing by the hospital nursery window. 10. her own baby had just died.

Quiz 35

1. the birth of John Ross. 2. Lucy. 3. Uncle Jock. 4. Patricia Shepard's boyfriend. 5. J. R.'s secretary; Louella. 6. she subtly encouraged it; she didn't want to lose J. R. as a son-in-law. 7. the company town house, owned by Ewing Oil, which became Kristin's private residence. 8. J. R. 9. Rudy Millington. 10. Alan Beam.

Quiz 36

1. neurofibromatosis. 2. it produces tumorous growths in the nervous system. 3. it creates progressive deterioration in adults but is generally fatal if it appears in infancy. 4. genetically. 5. Pam and Cliff's brother and sister who both died in infancy of neurofibromatosis. 6. no. 7. she didn't want to risk passing the disease along, and Bobby was anxious to start a family. 8. she feared John Ross had inherited the disease (through Cliff). 9. no (Cliff isn't his father). 10. no; Digger wasn't her biological father.

Quiz 37

1. Southeast Asia. 2. Vaughn Leland. 3. Southfork. 4. cheerleading. 5. Alan Beam. 6. two years. 7. she went insane. 8. when Jock was shot on a hunting trip and feared he might die, he made J. R. promise to take care of Amanda for him. 9. Louella; she was getting married and couldn't decide what to spend her money on. Bobby said newlyweds don't use living room furniture. 10. John Ross.

Quiz 38

1. Louisiana. 2. San Angelo. 3. Chicago. 4. Fort Worth. 5. Rome. 6. Paris. 7. Colorado. 8. New Orleans. 9. Corpus Christi. 10. Washington.

Quiz 39

1. Steven. 2. the annual Ewing-sponsored rodeo. 3. helped her pick up her shopping packages. 4. a restaurant. 5. 721 and 1701 were the hotel rooms where Dusty and Sue Ellen secretly met; 23 was the number of Dusty's apartment in Fort Worth. 6. she feared losing custody of John Ross (she was an alcoholic). 7. she heard a radio bulletin. 8. in Dusty's apartment. 9. she began drinking. 10. his plane crashed midway between San Angelo and Dallas.

Quiz 40

1. e. 2. g. 3. c. 4. h. 5. a. 6. d. 7. i. 8. j. 9. b. 10. f.

Quiz 41

1. Simon. 2. Wilbur Caulder; Hutch McKinney. 3. Cliff Barnes. 4. Beau Middens. 5. Matt Devlin. 6. Kristin. 7. Pam. 8. J. R.; Cliff. 9. Bobby. 10. Digger Barnes.

Quiz 42

1. he was dying of cancer. 2. Jenna Wade. 3. they spoke for the first time at the Ewing rodeo. 4. Dave's wife. 5. at Dallas airport. 6. *Madame Bovary*. 7. Mimosa Park. 8. Alan Beam. 9. Jordan Lee. 10. Alan Beam's girl friend on the sly.

Quiz 43

1. b. 2. a. 3. b. 4. b. 5. c. 6. c. 7. c. 8. c. 9. b. 10. c.

Quiz 44.

1. Bobby. 2. Vaughn Leland. 3. Cliff. 4. Sue Ellen. 5. Jock. 6. Hank Johnson. 7. Alan Beam. 8. Jordan Lee. 9. J. R. (to Miss Ellie). 10. Kristin.

Quiz 45

1. Leigh McCloskey. 2. Audrey Landers. 3. William Windom. 4. Priscilla Pointer. 5. Anne Francis. 6. Susan Flannery. 7. Monte Markham; 8. Joel Fabiani. 9. Fern Fitzgerald. 10. Craig Stevens.

Quiz 46

1. a cleaning woman; J. R. was sprawled on his back on the floor of the Ewing Oil reception area. 2. the first bullet bruised the kidney and injured the spleen; the second bullet was lodged in the spinal canal. 3. the police detective investigating the shooting. 4. the world-famous neurosurgeon summoned as a consultant on J. R.'s case. 5. Valene. 6. at the Sundowner Motel with her English instructor. 7. Sue Ellen. 8. spleen. 9. Kristin. 10. outside the Ewing office building. 11. Alan Beam. 12. Vaughn Leland; filing bankruptcy papers. 13. Jock; in a closet in J. R. and Sue Ellen's bedroom; two bullets were missing. 14. Sue Ellen. 15. Sue Ellen.

Quiz 47

1. J. R. had him fired from Smithfield and Bennett and then railroaded out of town. 2. J. R. was trying to send her back to the sanitarium. 3. J. R. had sabotaged Cliff's congressional race and closed down Ewing 23, an oil well in which Cliff was part owner. 4. J. R. was responsible for her husband's suicide. 5. J. R. was responsible for Leland going bankrupt. 6. J. R. tried to scare her out of town by having her picked up on a phony prostitution charge. 7. J. R. had separated her from her daughter many years ago. 8. J. R. had been partially responsible for one of her miscarriages; he was also ruining her marriage to Bobby and destroying her brother Cliff. 9. Lee and his friends had incurred substantial losses in J. R.'s Southeast Asian scam. 10. J. R. had driven first Gary and now Bobby from Southfork.

Quiz 48

1. her fingerprints were on the gun. 2. Kyle Bennett. 3. J. R. (Smithfield and Bennett might lose Ewing Oil as an account). 4. $100,000. 5. Cliff. 6. to Cliff's apartment. 7. to arrange for her to see John Ross. 8. in Kristin's apartment. 9. at Backman Park. 10. Miss Ellie and Pam.

Quiz 49

1. her whereabouts the night J. R. was shot. 2. by hypnosis. 3. to Dr. Ellby's office. 4. a cocktail lounge. 5. Kristin's apartment. 6. at Kristin's. 7. she was sure J. R. was there. 8. a drink. 9. in her car at the airport. 10. Kristin.

Quiz 50

1. Dusty Farlow. 2. November 21, 1980. 3. the actors' strike delayed the start of the 1980 fall TV season. 4. they were the only Lorimar staffers who knew who shot J. R. (Rich, Capice, and Katzman are the producers; Lewis and Marchetta are the

167

writers). 5. J. R. FOR PRESIDENT. 6. Jock. 7. it produced the sound of the bullets (a real gun was not fired). 8. George Bush. 9. Barbara Eden, his former *I Dream of Jeannie* co-star. 10. Kristin Shepard.

Quiz 51

1. parking valet. 2. a doctor. 3. he didn't—Lucy asked him. 4. Miss Ellie's (something old). 5. the Ewing condominium at Oakridge. 6. a junior executive position with Ewing Oil. 7. Clint Ogden. 8. a magnificent string of pearls (something new). 9. the handkerchief she'd held in her hand when she married Bobby. 10. a blue garter.

Quiz 52

1. medical textbooks. 2. Bobby. 3. Little John. 4. Leslie Stewart. 5. public relations. 6. computers. 7. a fishing and hunting resort. 8. they were married to men who lavished them with material possessions but loved power more. 9. Leslie Stewart; they were dining in a Japanese restaurant, and she was eating octopus. 10. because J. R. had used the other one once too often—particularly with Afton on Lucy's wedding day. 11. Bobby. 12. J. R.; in Southeast Asia.

Quiz 53

1. Port Aransas. 2. Sue Ellen; Clint Ogden. 3. cleaning woman. 4. detective; Dusty. 5. Donna. 6. Bobby. 7. J. R. 8. Louella. 9. a model. 10. soap box.

Quiz 54

1. c. 2. g. 3. j. 4. h. 5. b. 6. i. 7. f. 8. a. 9. e. 10. d.

Quiz 55

1. Ray Krebbs. 2. the death of her husband, Herbert Wentworth. 3. Leslie Stewart; J. R. could either divorce Sue Ellen or stay married. 4. Ray received a 25% share of the trust fund that Jock had set up for his sons. 5. Jock and Ellie. 6. Donna. 7. Dusty. 8. Lucy; to show Mitch she was a good homemaker. 9. in England during World War II. 10. very negative; he couldn't forgive her for abandoning him and Pam as children. 11. to divorce Jock. 12. he donated his own land as a wilderness preserve, so that Takapa might be developed into a resort.

Quiz 56

1. d. 2. i. 3. a. 4. f. 5. h. 6. j. 7. g. 8. c. 9. e. 10. b.

Quiz 57

1. Morgan Brittany. 2. Edward Winter. 3. Art Hindle. 4. Patricia McCormack. 5. Dennis Redfield. 6. Diane McBain. 7. Lindsay Bloom. 8. Jamie Wise. 9. Barry Nelson. 10. Gretchen Wyler.

Quiz 58

1. in the swimming pool at Southfork. 2. she fell from the balcony. 3. J. R. 4. that J. R. was innocent. 5. J. R.'s attorney. 6. heroin and PCP (angel dust). 7. accidental death. 8. J. R. 9. at the Southern Cross. 10. in Albuquerque.

Quiz 59

1. Miss Ellie's chili. 2. San Remo. 3. Pam. 4. he cried. 5. Cliff. 6. a chance to adopt a foreign child. 7. Rebecca. 8. he used the Heimlich maneuver on her (and saved her from

choking). 9. Afton's boss at the Stardrift Lounge. 10. Katherine's boyfriend in college.

Quiz 60
1. at Dallas airport (Sue Ellen was on her way to Kristin's funeral). 2. Jock. 3. by helicopter. 4. to kidnap John Ross just as the helicopter was about to leave; Miss Ellie refused. 5. Sue Ellen's divorce attorney. 6. by dwelling on her alcoholism and adultery. 7. since Sue Ellen and Dusty could never have a child together, John Ross would be her only offspring. 8. Sue Ellen's. 9. Sue Ellen. 10. to close down the Farlows' refineries and force them to trade John Ross for oil; 11. Sue Ellen. 12. $6,000 a month.

Quiz 61
1. plastic surgery. 2. Reunion Tower. 3. Brooktree. 4. medical research. 5. depression. 6. projection room. 7. South America; oil. 8. $2,000; Jeff Farraday; birth certificate. 9. Miss Ellie; Donna. 10. TV news reporter.

Quiz 62
1. b. 2. e. 3. f. 4. h. 5. j. 6. a. 7. d. 8. i. 9. g. 10. c

Quiz 63
1. c. 2. a. 3. f. 4. b. 5. h. 6. d. 7. i. 8. g. 9. j. 10. e.

Quiz 64
1. 30. 2. 20. 3. 20. 4. none. 5. none. 6. 10. 7. 10. 8. none (Gary later gave Lucy his 10 voting shares). 9. 10. 10. none.

Quiz 65

1. caterer. 2. Jock's, South America. 3. *Sam Culver, The Man and the Legend*. 4. Katherine. 5. Rebecca. 6. John Ross. 7. Barnes-Ewing feud. 8. Mitch. 9. Punk Anderson. 10. helicopter crash.

Quiz 66

1. J. R., Bobby, and Ray. 2. Miss Ellie. 3. Bobby. 4. to stay at Southfork till the men returned from South America. 5. Bobby. 6. Jock's necklace and medallion. 7. Ellie. 8. Pam. 9. J. R. 10. J. R. cried.

Quiz 67

1. an engagement ring. 2. Los Angeles. 3. she miscarried it. 4. Wellington field. 5. Marilee Stone. 6. by downing about 50 tranquilizers while he was drunk. 7. Afton. 8. Rebecca. 9. she fired J. R. as president of Ewing Oil. 10. remarry J. R.

Quiz 68

1. Christopher. 2. her father. 3. at Pam's exercise salon; Inga was an instructor there. 4. Roger Larson. 5. Austin. 6. Donna caught Ray and Bonnie in bed together there. 7. Stonehurst Oil. 8. he was a private detective who spied on Sue Ellen during her divorce from J. R. 9. she saw his wall filled with photos of her. 10. Jeff Farraday's corpse.

Quiz 69

1. Kate Reid. 2. Dale Robertson. 3. Ben Piazza. 4. Lois Chiles. 5. John Beck. 6. Donald Moffat. 7. Timothy Patrick Murphy. 8. Arlen Dean Snyder. 9. Albert Salmi. 10. John Reilly.

Quiz 70

1. at Dallas Memorial Hospital. 2. that she had refused to loan him the money he needed to avoid bankruptcy. 3. Afton. 4. took John Ross and all his belongings back to Southfork. 5. at one point he had stopped breathing and suffered loss of oxygen to the brain. 6. Afton. 7. Sue Ellen. 8. depression. 9. Pam. 10. Sue Ellen.

Quiz 71

1. her father died and left it to her. 2. 25%. 3. department heads at Ewing Oil. 4. J. R. was removed as president. 5. Miss Ellie, Lucy, and Bobby. 6. J. R. (voting for himself, Ray, and John Ross). 7. Jock's instructions stipulated that Miss Ellie could vote John Ross's shares only if the boy were not living at Southfork. 8. he had given J. R. his proxy. 9. Bobby. 10. he read every book on the bestseller list.

Quiz 72

1. d. 2. f. 3. j. 4. i. 5. g. 6. c. 7. h. 8. b. 9. e. 10. a.

Quiz 73

1. Clayton Farlow. 2. Pam. 3. Bobby. 4. J. R. 5. Afton. 6. Cliff. 7. she had purposely arranged to be in Galveston on a modeling assignment. 8. Pam; Cliff was getting drunk and she feared he'd make a scene. 9. he danced with Sue Ellen. 10. participated in the brawl that broke out. 11. J. R. 12. Cliff. 13. to make a deal about selling his gas stations. 14. oil tanks and refineries. 15. her second.

Quiz 74

1. he was an eyewitness to Jock's helicopter crash. 2. full title to Southfork and $50 million in assorted community

property holdings. 3. they each received $10 million from a special trust fund; however, Gary could only use the interest from his trust for the first four years after Jock's death. 4. handwritten; Punk Anderson. 5. one year; J. R. and Bobby would each control 50% of Ewing Oil assets. 6. 51% of the company. 7. 19% of the company. 8. the remaining 30% would be divided equally between Miss Ellie, Ray, and Gary. 9. $5 million. 10. the Ewings would have had to wait seven years before Jock could be declared legally dead.

Quiz 75

1. his tuxedo. 2. Sue Ellen remarried J. R. 3. Ray, Donna, Aunt Lil, and Mickey. 4. he mowed her lawn. 5. Ray and Donna (it was part of their plans for their cancelled trip to New York). 6. Leavenworth. 7. reckless driving. 8. to celebrate the fact that a court date had been set for Christopher's adoption. 9. Lucy; she was given access to her whole trust, while Gary's use of his money was severely restricted. 10. Cliff.

Quiz 76

1. d. 2. g. 3. f. 4. e. 5. i. 6. j. 7. h. 8. a. 9. c. 10 b.

Quiz 77

1. Mickey. 2. members of the Texas Energy Commission. 3. they agreed not to let it affect their friendship. 4. J. R. 5. Cliff. 6. J. R.. 7. she vowed to go to court and get Jock's will overturned and then to sell Ewing Oil. 8. hot chocolate. 9. his side of the bed is always empty after sunup. 10. her rape and abortion. 11. Mrs. Barnes. 12. neither; they were approximately the same age. 13. a bathing suit. 14. J. R. 15. *Talktime*.

Quiz 78

1. on the grounds that Jock was mentally incompetent when he wrote the codicil. 2. Pam. 3. J. R. and Bobby. 4. that Miss Ellie shouldn't interfere in the execution of the will. 5. because he had drawn up the will, he felt morally bound to defend it in court. 6. Clayton Farlow. 7. Gary and Ray. 8. Dave Culver; his "last hurrah." 9. a touch of jungle fever. 10. he upheld the will and the codicil and ruled against Miss Ellie.

Quiz 79

1. J. R. had forced Harwood Oil to cancel a military contract. 2. beautiful girls for hire. 3. Cliff. 4. her car was out of gas. 5. Afton. 6. that Pam would always protect Cliff. 7. George Hicks. 8. no. 9. Pam and Mark Graison; Katherine. 10. Walt Driscoll.

Quiz 80

1. she caught J. R. in bed with Holly Harwood. 2. it crashed against the stairway wall, ruining the wallpaper. 3. he blamed J. R. for the car accident that paralyzed Mickey. 4. to redo the wall that Sue Ellen had ruined; rolls of wallpaper. 5. he committed suicide. 6. while brawling, J. R. and Ray knocked over candles, and the wallpaper caught on fire. 7. John Ross and Sue Ellen. 8. the doctor had sedated her. 9. on a trip with Clayton. 10. Bobby.

Quiz 81

1. Chris Atkins. 2. Alexis Smith. 3. Martin E. Brooke. 4. Joanna Miles. 5. Glenn Corbett. 6. Daniel Pilon. 7. James Brown. 8. Priscilla Beaulieu Presley. 9. Shalane McCall. 10. Richard Jaeckel.

Quiz 82

1. at Billy Bob's; she was working as a waitress. 2. on a cruise of the Mediterranean and the Greek Isles. 3. Quorum Hotel. 4. Cotton Bowl. 5. New York. 6. agree to end their marriage. 7. Houston; in Atlanta visiting her brother. 8. Sue Ellen and Peter Richards. 9. in Malibu Beach, California; Katherine. 10. Miss Ellie and Clayton.

Quiz 83

1. he holds the mortgage on her boutique. 2. 13. 3. she owns (it's a condominium). 4. he's an Italian count. 5. he favors it enthusiastically. 6. Jenna announced to Pam that she and Bobby were engaged. 7. as a waitress she liked the idea of being waited on for a change. 8. by kissing Bobby in public. 9. her father lost it through bad business deals. 10. by revealing that Bobby was not Charlie's father.

Quiz 84

1. Pam's inordinate concern for the Ewings after the Southfork fire. 2. Mark's jet-set ex-girlfriend. 3. at the charity rodeo, Tracy would contribute $5,000 a point if Mark topped last year's score; otherwise, Mark would contribute $5,000 a point. 4. he injured his knee playing tennis with Pam. 5. he considered it too risky and opposed it. 6. polo. 7. Graisco. 8. Dr. Jerry Kenderson (Mark's doctor). 9. he crashed his plane over the Gulf of Mexico. 10. a letter, written by Mark, explaining why he chose to die and reiterating his love for her.

Quiz 85

1. that her mastectomy would bother him. 2. Amy. 3. Jessica Montford; father unknown. 4. Miss Ellie. 5. J. R. 6. to a fashion show at the Quorum Hotel; Donna. 7. he read Jessica's diary. 8. Jessica. 9. Clayton. 10. Sue Ellen and Ray.

Quiz 86

1. he was John Ross's camp counselor. 2. psychology. 3. so he and Sue Ellen would have a private place to meet. 4. Sue Ellen didn't know. 5. Peter's former college roommate. 6. J. R. 7. in Peter's car. 8. if Sue Ellen would return to his bedroom permanently. 9. she reluctantly agreed. 10. he threatened to kill J. R.

Quiz 87

1. his life-support system was disconnected. 2. Aunt Lil. 3. Paul Morgan. 4. Percy McManus. 5. no. 6. prosecution. 7. Sue Ellen was with him; Walt Driscoll was the other driver. 8. J. R. Walt Driscoll purposely rammed the car, believing J. R. was in it. 9. Ray and Bobby (for setting up Driscoll's arrest). 10. $500,000. 11. he was a corporate attorney. 12. no. 13. no. 14. yes. 15. five years in the state penitentiary (suspended) and 18 months' probation.

Quiz 88

1. Clayton Farlow. 2. Mark; Jenna. 3. Cliff Barnes. 4. development of the Tundra Torque drill bit. 5. he praised Digger Barnes and damned Jock Ewing. 6. they were the first recipients of the Jock Ewing Memorial Scholarship. 7. Peter. 8. Pam, Jenna, Katherine, Afton, and Sue Ellen. 9. Cliff. 10. Alcoholics Anonymous. 11. Peter's. 12. Cliff. 13. Bobby had asked Jenna to the ball instead of her. 14. Punk Anderson. 15. Cliff.

Quiz 89

1. f. 2. h. 3. g. 4. c. 5. i. 6. d. 7. a. 8. j. 9. e. 10. b.

Quiz 90

1. Cody's Bar and Grill. 2. Dallas Memorial Hospital. 3. Gold Lakes Sanitarium. 4. Windsor Meadows. 5. Madame Claude's Salon. 6. Prairie Motel. 7. Billy Bob's. 8. SMU. 9. Oil Barons' Club. 10. Missing River.

Quiz 91

1. d. 2. i. 3. h. 4. f. 5. j. 6. c. 7. k. 8. a. 9. b. 10. l. 11. e. 12. g.

Quiz 92

1. Dugan. 2. sergeant. 3. Andy Sampson; to repair the damage to the house after the fire. 4. Deputy Assistant Secretary of the Interior for the Outer Continental Shelf. 5. auditors who tallied J. R.'s and Bobby's profits to determine who won control of Ewing Oil. 6. Peter Richards'. 7. London. 8. Donna. 9. it was one of Peter's affectionate names for John Ross. 10. Tracy Anders, referring to Mark Graison. 11. John Ross's teacher. 12. $157 million. 13. Jenna's father. 14. her late husband's regimental sword. 15. Charlie's horse.

Quiz 93

1. J. R. 2. Bobby. 3. Ray. 4. Peter. 5. Cliff. 6. Clint. 7. Jock. 8. Alan. 9. Clayton. 10. Bobby.

Quiz 94

1. Marilee Stone. 2. Pam. 3. Donna. 4. Gary Ewing. 5. Lucy. 6. Cliff. 7. Jenna Wade. 8. Miss Ellie. 9. Ray. 20. Rebecca Wentworth.

Quiz 95

1. Ed Haynes. 2. Ray. 3. Mark Graison. 4. Alex Ward. 5. Ben Maxwell. 6. Christopher. 7. Taylor "Guzzler" Bennett. 8. Harrison Page. 9. Luke Middens. 10. Bobby.

Quiz 96

1. alcoholism. 2. literary careers. 3. membership in the DOA (and marriage to oil men). 4. engagements to Lucy. 5. Cliff's former secretaries. 6. died in plane crashes. 7. illegitimately fathered. 8. abandoned by their mothers. 9. own oil companies. 10. named Linda.

Quiz 97

1. Peter Richards. 2. Jessica Montford. 3. Miss Ellie. 4. Pam and Lucy. 5. Roger Larson. 6. Jock. 7. J. R. 8. Mitch Cooper. 9. Cliff (or Bobby). 10. Pam.

Quiz 98

1. g. 2. i. 3. a. 4. h. 5. j. 6. b. 7. e. 8. d. 9. c. 10. f.

Quiz 99

1. d. 2. g. 3. j. 4. h. 5. b. 6. i. 7. c. 8. a. 9. e. 10. f.

Quiz 100

1. i. 2. a. 3. f. 4. j. 5. g. 6. c. 7. e. 8. d. 9. h. 10. b.

Quiz 101

1. e. 2. a. 3. f. 4. g. 5. c. 6. i. 7. j. 8. b. 9. h. 10. d.

Quiz 102

1. worked as waitresses. 2. Anderson is their last name. 3. both had psychotic sisters. 4. attorneys. 5. each assumed he had fathered Kristin's baby. 6. temporarily confined to wheelchairs. 7. murdered. 8. kidnapped. 9. suffered miscarriages. 10. shared the name Farraday; Christopher's father was Jeff Farraday; Pam's husband's middle name was Farraday.

Quiz 103

1. false. 2. true. 3. false. 4. true. 5. true. 6. false. 7. true. 8. true. 9. false. 10. true.

Quiz 104

1. true. 2. false. 3. true. 4. false. 5. false. 6. true. 7. false. 8. true. 9. true. 10. true.

Quiz 105

1. false. 2. true. 3. true. 4. true. 5. false. 6. false. 7. false. 8. false. 9. true. 10 true.

Quiz 106

1. Katherine. 2. Sam Culver's diary. 3. phony codicil to Jock's will, written by J. R. 4. authentic codicil to Jock's will, written by Jock in South America. 5. Jessica Montford's diary. 6. Mark Graison's last letter to Pam. 7. Jock's letter of instructions, written in South America. 8. ransom note written by Bobby's kidnappers. 9. message left by Julie Grey on Cliff's answering machine. 10. written by Cliff and signed by Katherine.

Quiz 107

1: Sly. 2. Bobby. 3. Charlie Wade. 4. Marvin. 5. Gary. 6. Edison Farraday Haynes. 7. Mickey (Trotter). 8. Dave Stratton (Cliff's friend). 9. John Ross Ewing. 10. Christopher.

Quiz 108

1. both were shot. 2. bankers. 3. Frank is their first name. 4. both have daughters. 5. singers. 6. both loved Jock Ewing. 7. Leslie Stewart's lovers. 8. Sue Ellen's mom and Mitch's mom—probably the only two women in Dallas (aside from Miss Ellie) who actually *liked* J. R. 9. both men kidnapped Lucy. 10. Southfork ranch hands.

Quiz 109

1. male. 2. male. 3. female. 4. male. 5. female. 6. male. 7. female. 8. male. 9. male. 10. female.

Quiz 110

1. Galveston. 2. England. 3. Canada. 4. the South of France. 5. Puerto Rico. 6. Cuba. 7. Paris. 8. California. 9. Houston. 10. New York

Quiz 111

1. J. R.; Cliff; Ray. 2. J. R.; Cliff. 3. J. R. 4. J. R.; Cliff. 5. J. R. 6. Ray. 7. J. R.; Ray. 8. J. R.; Cliff. 9. none. 10. J. R.

Quiz 112

1. J. R. 2. Bobby. 3. J. R. 4. J. R. 5. J. R. 6. Bobby. 7. J. R. 8. Bobby. 9. Bobby. 10. Bobby.

Quiz 113
1. John Ross. 2. John Ross. 3. Christopher (Katherine). 4. Christopher. 5. both. 6. Christopher. 7. John Ross. 8. John Ross. 9. Christopher. 10. John Ross.

Quiz 114
1. Rebecca. 2. both. 3. both. 4. both. 5. neither. 6. both. 7. Rebecca. 8. Ellie (Rebecca was already deceased). 9. neither. 10. Ellie.

Quiz 115
1. Sue Ellen. 2. Pam. 3. Pam. 4. Pam. 5. Sue Ellen. 6. Pam. 7. Pam. 8. Sue Ellen. 9. Sue Ellen. 10. Pam.

Quiz 116
1. Ray. 2. Gary. 3. Gary. 4. Ray. 5. Ray. 6. Ray. 7. Gary. 8. Ray. 9. Ray. 10. Gary.

Quiz 117
1. Julie. 2. Sly. 3. Kristin. 4. Sly. 5. Sly. 6. Kristin. 7. Julie. 8. Sly. 9. Sly. 10. Sly.

Quiz 118
1. Rebecca's children. 2. Ellie's grandchildren. 3. attempted suicide. 4. independent oil company owners. 5. Jock's sons. 6. attorneys. 7. lived in condos in Dallas. 8. widows. 9. spent time in psychiatric institutions. 10. all worked at the Store.

Quiz 119

1. Mitch. 2. Mickey. 3. Mickey (at J. R. and Sue Ellen's wedding reception Mickey told J. R. that Cliff was dancing with Sue Ellen). 4. Mitch. 5. Mickey. 6. Mitch. 7. Mitch. 8. Mickey. 9. Mitch. 10. Mickey.

Quiz 120

1. Jock. 2. Clayton. 3. both (Gary and Dusty). 4. both. 5. Clayton. 6. Clayton. 7. neither. 8. both. 9. neither. 10. both.

Quiz 121

1. Boyd. 2. Leland. 3. McLeish. 4. Smithfield. 5. York. 6. Beam. 7. Danvers. 8. Krebbs. 9. Sullivan. 10. McKinney. 11. Culver. 12. Lee. 13. Thurman. 14. Driscoll. 15. Garr. 16. Southworth. 17. Elrod. 18. Farraday. 19. Randolph. 20. Bennett.

Quiz 122

1. Afton. 2. both. 3. Lucy. 4. Lucy. 5. neither. 6. neither. 7. Afton. 8. both. 9. Lucy. 10. Lucy.

Quiz 123

1. Charlene Tilton. 2. Morgan Fairchild. 3. Fern Fitzgerald. 4. Priscilla Pointer. 5. Joan Van Ark. 6. Barbara Bel Geddes. 7. Audrey Landers. 8. Victoria Principal (technically, since Pam was in the opening scene of the first show). 9. Tina Louise. 10. Mary Crosby.

Quiz 124

1. Jared Martin. 2. Patrick Duffy (technically, since Bobby

was in the opening scene of the first show). 3. Leigh McCloskey. 4. John Beck. 5. Keenan Wynn. 6. George O. Petrie. 7. Steve Kanaly. 8. Ken Kercheval. 9. Morgan Woodward. 10. Jim Davis.

Quiz 125
1. no. 2. no. 3. yes. 4. yes. 5. no. 6. no. 7. yes. 8. yes. 9. yes. 10. no.

Quiz 126
1. yes. 2. no. 3. yes. 4. no. 5. yes. 6. yes. 7. no. 8. yes. 9. no. 10. no.

Quiz 127
1. no. 2. yes. 3. yes. 4. no. 5. yes. 6. no. 7. yes. 8. yes. 9. no. 10. yes.

Quiz 128
1. one million. 2. Sly. 3. Argentina. 4. by private jet. 5. Jessica; Ellie and Clayton's wedding day. 6. Punk and Mavis Anderson. 7. editor of a fashion magazine, waitress, boutique owner. 8. Katherine; Renaldo Marchetta. 9. a mild concussion. 10. 10.

Quiz 129
1. c. 2. e. 3. a. 4. g. 5. h. 6. b. 7. f. 8. d.

Quiz 130

1. Friday, Saturday, and Sunday. 2. Ted Shackelford and Joan Van Ark (*Knots Landing*). 3. Dr. Rudy Wells. 4. Donna Reed (Donna Stone was her character name on the long-running *Donna Reed Show*); 5. Mel. Ferrer who played Harrison Page on *Dallas*, later became Phillip Erikson on *Falcon Crest*. 6. Veronica Hamel (Leann Rees, Pam's friend). 7. 30. 8. Barry Nelson played Sue Ellen's lawyer, Arthur Elrod; Barbara Bel Geddes played Sue Ellen's mother-in-law, Miss Ellie. 9. Victoria Principal and Steve Kanaly. 10. Larry Hagman (Fort Worth, Texas).

Quiz 131

1. Peter Richards. 2. Jessica. 3. J. R. 4. Charlie. 5. Katherine. 6. Clayton. 7. Cliff; Julie Grey; J. R.; Bobby. 8. Vaughn Leland. 9. Mark Graison. 10. Jessica; Cliff.

Quiz 132

1. Gold Canyon 340. 2. $54 million. 3. blindness. 4. Pam. 5. Jenna. 6. to see if J. R.'s phone was bugged. 7. Afton. 8. Sue Ellen and John Ross. 9. he read it in the *Dallas Press*. 10. Lucy's friend Muriel.

Quiz 133

1. yes. 2. nobody; they responded to a call from Southfork's automatic fire alarm system. 3. Pam and Bobby's impending divorce. 4. she heard a radio report. 5. he was conscious for several weeks after the accident, then became comatose. 6. he was paralyzed from the neck down. 7. Christopher, because Cliff never had time to visit his nephew. 8. sunglasses. 9. by covering most of the letter and telling Pam it was a routine business letter from Wentworth corporate headquarters. 10. Pam's lawyer; that Pam no longer loved Bobby.

Quiz 134

1. shyness. 2. Lucy. 3. he was Sam Culver's legal counsel.
4. Mark, Pam, Cliff, and Afton. 5. Serena. 6. Pam was
present, Bobby was not. 7. rotten luck with men. 8. Aunt
Maggie. 9. Cliff. 10. Jenna.

Quiz 135

1. the night of the charity contest at Billy Bob's. 2. Houston.
3. Cliff and Pam. 4. took the phone off the hook. 5. Pam,
Donna, and Jenna. 6. Sue Ellen. 7. Pam (as an oil executive).
8. Renaldo Marchetta. 9. Bobby and J. R. 10. John Ross.

Quiz 136

1. houses for sale in Dallas (Clayton was in the process of
moving there). 2. $25 million. 3. Ray and Donna. 4. town
house. 5. Jordan Lee. 6. Office of Land Management. 7.
Pam. 8. so she could personally deliver her book manuscript
to her publisher. 9. Dr. Adrian Krane. 10. aboard her yacht.

Quiz 137

1. riding the range on the Southern Cross. 2. discipline. 3.
Sue Ellen's reconciliation with J. R. 4. Punk Anderson. 5.
for stealing a car. 6. the surviving brother would have gained
both the winner's and loser's share of Ewing stock. 7. a long
life. 8. that the business must always be run by a member of
the family. 9. Sue Ellen and Marilee Stone. 10. tending the
stables.

Quiz 138

1. the hairdresser's. 2. Harry McSween. 3. Cliff. 4. on a
Caribbean trip. 5. the Tuxedo Club. 6. to Braddock for a few

beers. 7. lemonade. 8. the frozen ground. 9. his chain of cut-rate gas stations. 10. in a coffee shop; breakfast.

Quiz 139

1. J. R.'s appearance on Roy Ralston's show. 2. J. R. 3. $30 million. 4. if J. R. could use Clayton's refinery to store his excess oil. 5. to find out something about George Hicks that Bobby could use to blackmail him. 6. cocaine. 7. he found out that Afton had slept with Gil Thurman. 8. the Houston refinery owner whom Rebecca was on her way to see when her plane crashed. 9. Pam (when she left Bobby). 10. in Cliff's town house.

Quiz 140

1. Howard Keel. 2. Patrick Duffy. 3. Christopher Atkins. 4. Charlene Tilton. 5. Barbara Bel Geddes. 6. Lois Chiles. 7. John Beck. 8. Linda Gray. 9. Steve Kanaly. 10. Victoria Principal.

Quiz 141

1. the weekly shopping list. 2. a note explaining Mickey Trotter's car accident. 3. Cliff (it's the name of the condominium development he lives in). 4. British. 5. Holly. 6. lipstick on the collar of J. R.'s shirt. 7. $17 million. 8. $40 million. 9. in Clayton's hotel suite. 10. the Canadian oil fields Bobby had invested in.

Quiz 142

1. half-brothers. 2. mother and daughter. 3. half-sisters. 4. husband and wife. 5. formerly stepmother and stepson. 6. grandmother and granddaughter. 7. half-brother and half-

sister. 8. brother and sister. 9. uncle and niece. 10. sister-in-law and brother-in-law.

Quiz 143

1. d (Bobby). 2. h (Lucy). 3. i (Pam). 4. c (Digger). 5. b (Ellie). 6. a (John Ross). 7. e (J. R.). 8. g (Cliff). 9. j (Evelyn). 10. f (Amanda).

Quiz 144

1. Bobby's offer to buy a boutique for her. 2. Clayton and Jessica. 3. geologicals of the most desirable offshore oil tracts. 4. to be John Ross's private counselor. 5. leukemia. 6. Pam and Christopher. 7. Donna. 8. Edgar Randolph. 9. Cliff's secretary. 10. Ray.

About the Author

JASON BONDEROFF is the Editorial Director of *Daytime TV* magazine, and the author of a number of celebrity biographies, including TOM SELLECK, ALAN ALDA (also available in Signet paperback) BARBARA WALTERS, DONAHUE! and BROOKE.